PN
3241
F24

INTER·FOLIA·FRUCTUS

ANDREW DICKSON WHITE

D1262021

Cornell University Library

PN 3241.F24

Passion play at Ober-Ammergau,

3 1924 027 190 572

THE PASSION PLAY

THE PASSION PLAY

AT

OBER-AMMERGAU

WITH THE WHOLE DRAMA TRANSLATED INTO ENGLISH, AND THE
SONGS OF THE CHORUS, IN GERMAN AND ENGLISH

BY

THE AUTHOR OF "CHARLES LOWDER"

[Maria Trench]

"Tibi reddetur votum."—PS. lxv. 1

LONDON:
W. H. ALLEN & CO., 13, WATERLOO PLACE, S.W.
AND CALCUTTA

1890

CORNELL UNIVERSITY.
The
President White
Library
RECEIVED 1891.

A. 9382.

LONDON:
PRINTED BY WOODFALL AND KINDER,
70 TO 76, LONG ACRE, W.C.

TO THE

Memory

OF

THE VENERABLE GEISTLICHER RATH

DAISENBERGER

AND OF

MY FRIEND AND COMPANION AT OBER-AMMERGAU

IN 1880

MARGARET LEIGHTON.

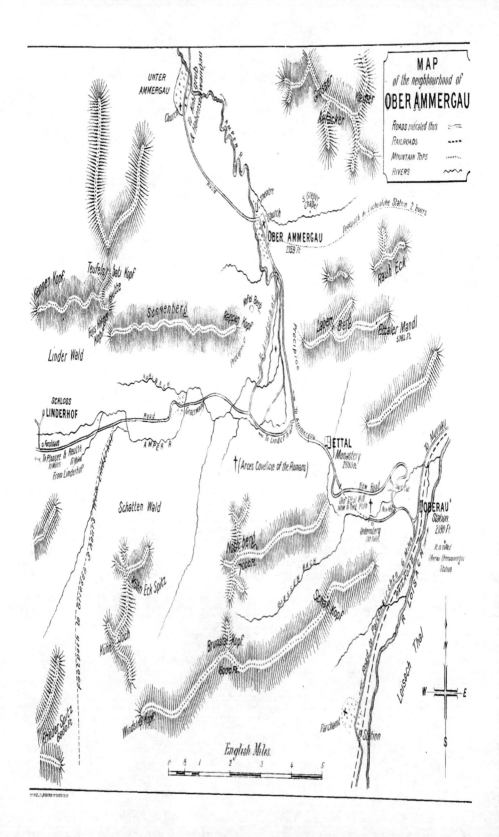

INTRODUCTION.

THE whole dialogue of the Passion Play at Ober-Ammergau trans-lated into English, with the' Choruses, and an account of the perform-ance, is, we believe, given for the first time in the following pages. The general account of the Play, and of a visit to Ober-Ammergau, were written in 1880, soon after witnessing two representations, in the month of August. At that time the words of the drama had never been published, nor, I imagine, even printed ; at least the separate parts, which some of the actors showed us in their cottages, were in manuscript.

The impossibility of obtaining any *libretto* of the Play has hitherto been so great a loss, especially to those who cannot readily follow the German dialogue, that it is hoped this little book will supply a real need. In 1880 nothing was given of the actual words in the various Handbooks sold in the village or at Munich, except the Choruses, and an English translation of them. This latter was in rhyme, to which accuracy of translation was, certainly, in great measure sacrificed. It is so important to give as closely as possible the exact words in English of the German, that, while observing measure, rhyme has not been attempted in the following translations, which are entirely new and original. But it will be seen that almost every English line represents the corresponding German line, and this has been done for the benefit especially of those who do not know German, in order to convey to them, as nearly as possible, the somewhat rugged strength and spirit of the original.

It is hardly necessary to say that this celebrated religious play is acted in fulfilment, according to tradition, of a solemn vow made by the villagers in 1633, that if Almighty God would remove a pestilence raging amongst them, they would perform the Passion Tragedy in thanksgiving every tenth year. It had already, probably, been well known amongst them as one of the "Mysteries" frequently acted in the Middle Ages. The vow has been faithfully observed, but the performances were cut short in 1870 by the Franco-German War; many of the actors, amongst them Mayr, being called to serve in the Bavarian Army. It was repeated in 1871 as an act of thanksgiving for the peace, and the last performance was in 1880.

The shortest route at that time from Munich was by rail to Mürnau, and from thence by road, a drive of about four hours, to Ober-Ammergau. The railway is now open from Mürnau to Partenkirchen, and the station of "Oberau-Ober-Ammergau" is within an hour and a half on foot from the village of the Passion Play. The old steep road (described at pp. 1, 2) exists no longer, except as a foot-path. A magnificent new road, one long zig-zag, has been made, and was opened in 1889. It turns off to the right from the old road, half-way between Oberau Station and the foot of the Ettal Hill, and winds up the mountain, crossing the old road not far from the top, and, entering it again half-way between the top of the hill and Ettal, follows the old Augsburg mule-track. This new road is of course the best for carriages. For pedestrians who wish to avoid the old steep hill, there is a short cut, just after crossing a little stream about 200 yards from the beginning of the new road, which leads into it again in about a quarter of an hour, avoiding the long zig-zag, and about a mile and a half of road.

A very pretty route to Ammergau, for those who have time, is by the Black Forest and Lake of Constance to Lindau, thence to Sonthofen, by road to Reutte, and by the Plansee and Ammerwald to Linderhof and Ammergau. The Palaces of Hohenschwangau and Neu-Schwanstein can be visited from Reutte, and Linderhof Palace *en route* from Reutte to Ammergau. A longer journey by rail brings the traveller from Lindau to Füssen, two miles from Hohenschwangau. The scenery is lovely, and is out of the way for those going on to Innspruck or Salzburg from Ammergau.

The Ettal Monastery, on the route first mentioned, is worthy of note, and is, Mr. Jackson says, in his Album of the Passion Play, "one of the many wonderful sites of incomparable beauty which the sons of St. Benedict were wont to select for their abode." The abbots were feudal lords over Ammergau, and the monks must have exercised a large influence over the villagers, as well as those of the monastery of Rothen-buch, under whose pastoral care they lived, and who served the Church of Ammergau. Mr. Jackson tells us that both the monks of Ettal and Rothenbuch certainly had religious plays of their own ; " for in 1803, when the property of the suppressed Bavarian monasteries was put up for auction, costumes used in these plays were sold, and the community of Ober-Ammergau purchased from Ettal a number of dresses, some of which they still turn to use."*

Ettal monastery was founded in 1330 by the German Emperor, Ludwig the Bavarian, as a shrine for an image of the Madonna, given to him by a monk when in great peril from enemies at Milan, with a promise of deliverance if he would bind himself to build a Benedictine monastery in the valley of the Ammer, and place in it the image. The whole buildings were destroyed by lightning in 1744, the prior saving the image at the risk of his life, and, although rebuilt, this image is almost the only relic of its former treasures, since the ruin of monastic bodies in Bavaria in 1803.

Entering Ammergau from Ettal, the curious peak of the Kofel, sur-mounted by a large cross, appears to guard the village, and the immense marble crucifix, erected by the late King of Bavaria in remembrance of the Play of 1871, is a prominent object. The sort of gorge through which the road passes, just before reaching Ammergau, was called *Arces Covelicæ*, hence the name Kofel. It is said that on being invited to take their Play to England or America the Ammergauers replied :—" We will willingly do so, but we must take with us the whole village, and its guardian genius, the Kofel."

The trade of the village, wood-carving, must have largely contributed to their artistic power. There is a school of design both at Partenkirchen, assisted by a State grant, and at Ammergau ; and the three men who represented the "Christus" since 1850 have all been wood-carvers, chiefly of crucifixes and other religious subjects. Lechner, admirable both for his moral and religious character and real genius as an actor, is also a skilful wood-carver. Besides this, they are educated by their Church ceremonies. The scene of Christ's entry into Jerusalem is, Mr. Jackson says, "for the most part a repetition of the Church Procession on Palm

---

* The dresses of the chief actors are made by the tailor of the " Hof-Theater" at Munich. Pilate's dress cost 200 marks, and that of Caiaphas 175.

Sunday, even to the singing of the beautiful chorale ' Hail to Thee, Hail, O David's Son!' so that the people dramatically display on the Passion stage very much of what they have imbibed in Church." The stage is also left standing when the rest of the theatre is taken down at the close of the decennial performance, and there the villagers are trained by acting various plays, secular as well as religious ; many of them written by their late venerable pastor, Daisenberger. He gave his whole life to the direction of his people in elevating and ennobling their performance. "I undertook the labour," he said, "with the best will, for the love of my Divine Redeemer, and with only one object in view, namely, the edification of the Christian world." As the Play is to the villagers a religious act, it is not unsuitable that Sundays should be chosen for its performance.

The plan of the theatre which we give is of that used in 1880, but we are informed that a larger one is being erected this year. The following is a list of the principal performers in the Play of 1890. Those marked † took the same parts in 1871 and 1880 :—

PASSION PLAY, 1890.

CHRISTUS	Joseph Mayr†.
PETRUS	Jacob Hett†.
JUDAS	Johann Zwink (in 1871 and 1880, JOHN).
JOHANNES	Peter Rendl.
MARIA	Rosa Lang.
MAGDALENA	Amalia Deschler.
MARTHA	Helena Lang.
JOSEPH OF ARIMATHEA .	Martin Oppenrieder†.
NICODEMUS	Franz Steinbacher†.
CAIAPHAS	Burgmeister Johann Lang†.
ANNAS	Franz Rutz, senr.
PILATUS	Thomas Rendl†.
HERODES	Johann Diemer (in 1871 and 1880, CHORAGUS).
BARABBAS	Johann Oswald.
NATHANIEL	Sebastian Lang†.
EZEKIEL	Rochus Lang†.
RABBI ARCHOLAUS . .	Sebastian Bauer.
SIMON CYRENIAN . . .	Gregor Lechner (in 1871 and 1880, JUDAS).
CHORAGUS	Jacob Rutz.

Leader of the Orchestra, Josef Gruber.

Lechner's rendering of the part of Judas was *the* acting in the Play,* and it is a matter of great regret that he should not be given the same part this year. He is himself terribly disappointed, and as he feels perfectly able to act the part, he might have had the chance, we imagine, with Zwink in reserve in case he failed. Diemer, the former Choragus, is afraid to take that part on account of chest weakness, and is, we are told, "worthily succeeded by Jacob Rutz."

For much of the information given here, the writer is indebted to Colonel Ward, who has made his home at Partenkirchen, and is long and intimately acquainted with the principal Ammergauers. He will permit this acknowledgment of his great kindness in taking trouble to collect and impart trustworthy information.

A letter from Mayr, the "Christus," gives the following dates for the performances in 1890, "provided," he says, "no alterations occur":—

Whitsun Monday, May 26.
June 1, 8, 15, 16, 22, 25, 29.
July 6, 13, 20, 23, 27.
August 3, 6, 10, 17, 20, 24, 31.
September 3, 7, 14, 21, 28.

"If, on the appointed days for the representation," Mayr adds, "the throng of kind visitors be such that the theatre cannot hold the whole number of them, the Passion Play will be repeated on the day following in the same complete manner."

A meeting was held two months ago at Ammergau to draw up an official statement as to prices for board and lodging, tickets, &c., which the older villagers are desirous to have published in the English newspapers, in order to prevent any imposition or traffic in tickets. It is to be hoped that this will be done, for as people from all parts of the world throng more and more to the Passion Play, it becomes difficult to hinder much which is most to be regretted. Already, we are told, the village is full of people, photographers, confectioners, &c., offering fabulous prices for shops. Meanwhile, it may be said that rooms are fixed at 3*s.* per day generally, but that they will be from 2*s.* to 5*s.*—a poor room 2*s.*, a very good large one 5*s.* Board, which was in 1880 4*s.* per day, will be somewhat higher, owing to increased prices, meat alone being more than double the price that it cost in 1882.

* *See* pp. 11, 12, 13, 15, 21, 22.

The best way to secure rooms, and tickets (which are given with the rooms in order to avoid traffic in them), is to apply to the Committee, or to the Burgermeister. Two months' notice would probably be sufficient. There is to be an English Chaplain (S.P.G.) at Ammergau this year, from Whitsunday until the last of the performances, who will have early celebrations ; and there is also a Chaplain for the charming English Church at Partenkirchen, a most lovely spot, about six miles from Ammergau, on the road to Innspruck. This latter village would be a delightful spot in which to pass the summer : we much regretted, when passing through it in 1880, that we could not spend some time there.

It has been thought best, in this volume, not to interrupt the " Text of the Passion Drama " by descriptions or criticisms, but for these to refer the reader to the corresponding pages in the first part.

Of the chief actors two have passed away since 1880—Tobias Flunger* (Christus in 1850, Pilate in 1860 and 1871) and Johann Allinger (Barabbas). The latter died in 1888, Flunger in January 1887.

But the greatest, the irreparable loss to Ammergau and to the Passion Play, is that of the venerable Daisenberger,† who died April 20, 1883. He published in 1879 an excellent little book, containing a topographical and historical description of his parish.‡ The concluding words of his preface may fitly find place here :—

" May strangers, who come here to the Holy Play, become more closely acquainted and in closer friendship with Ammergau through the perusal of these pages, and also oftentimes after their return to their homes, renew within themselves the memory of this still mountain valley.

---

* He was sixty-four in 1880. " My grandfather," he said, " was a day-labourer, and played the Apostle Thomas. My father was a carver, and in 1820 was one of the Executioners ; later on he was always a Pharisee. I myself was, in 1820, amongst the people ; in 1830 I sang in the Chorus as ' Schutzgeist'; 1840 I was second violin in the orchestra ; 1850 I was Christus ; 1860, 1870–71 Pilate ; and now I am an Apostle, and Moses in the Tableaux. My daughter Franciska was ' Mutter-Gottes ' in 1870–71, and my second daughter was ' Schutzgeist' the same year." Flunger was one of the best men at Ammergau.

† *See* pp. 3, 32.

‡ " Historisch-topographische Beschreibung der Pfarrei Ober-Ammergau." He gave the copyright to his two nephews, George Gastl and Sebastian Lang (from whom it may be bought at Ammergau, price 1½ mark), with the stipulation that to the villagers it should be sold at cost price.

"And you, beloved community and fellow-parishioners, may you, through this perusal, be strengthened anew in the attachment to your birthplace, and in the resolve to resist carefully all which would tend to the hurt or dishonour of the same, and ever faithfully to work together for all whereby the well-being and the good name of Ammergau shall be furthered, concord and unity stedfastly preserved in your dwellings, and whereby true Christian piety and morality shall blossom into ever fairer flower and fruit!

"And may you look upon this present description as a spiritual legacy, if I may say so, of your old friend, teacher, pastor,* and still keep for him a friendly memory even after his death!"

* Seelsorger.

NOTE.—Tickets for the Passion Play can only be secured beforehand by those who take rooms from the villagers, when they are supplied with the rooms. Visitors staying at hotels (which have been mostly bought up by speculators), cannot buy tickets until the morning of each performance, at the entrance to the theatre.

Letters to the Committee, etc., should be written in English, except by good German scholars. One of the villagers has been in England for three or four years, and knows English perfectly; and Mayr's two daughters know enough of it to understand what is wanted. Mayr has been entirely unable to understand some of the letters already written to him, in imperfectly expressed German.

DESCRIPTION

OF

THE PASSION PLAY

AND OF

A VISIT TO OBER-AMMERGAU IN 1880

THE PASSION PLAY.

THE traveller from Munich to Innsbruck leaves on the right, about two hours before reaching Partenkirchen, the steep mountain of Ettal. The road by which it is ascended was formerly the only route between Italy and Augsburg, by which the merchants of the latter town carried on their commerce. It was also the Roman Road. Its steepness makes the ascent a real obstacle to intercourse between the world and the valley to which it leads; while the remarkable Benedictine monastery, now secularised, which crowns its summit, and is, as it were, the gate to the Ammer-Thal, has been a centre of moral and religious influences and culture to its inhabitants. Here in 1760 Franz Zwink, the peasant painter, acted as colour mixer to the renowed Martin Knoller during his work in the convent church, and, returning to his home, covered the cottage walls of Ammergau with frescoes full of talent and vigour, and of such excellence in colouring that where they have been preserved, as on the Burgermeister's house, they are still fresh and brilliant, in spite of exposure to weather. Most have perished in the frequent fires which take place in the village, or in consequence of houses being pulled down and altered. Martin Knoller was a direct descendant of the great colourists of the sixteenth and seventeenth centuries, and it has been well said, with regard to Zwink's work, that it is as though a wandering wave from the mighty sea of the Renaissance had broken into this lonely mountain valley. At Ettal, too, the convent-bred Dedler, the organist of Ober-Ammergau, and author of the music of the Passion Play, must have found a congenial home; and here Daisenberger, for thirty years parish priest of Ammergau, in 1880 venerable and revered in his retirement, studied and tarried for a time.

Up this steep ascent we slowly toiled, on Thursday, August 12, in the year of Grace 1880. We had engaged an "Einspänner" at Mürnau, which just held two, with our very small luggage strapped behind. But all travellers were expected to walk up this Hill of Difficulty, and indeed the road was more like a ladder laid straight against the side of the mountain than anything else. It made the approach to Ober-Ammergau a real pilgrimage to those not robust, and we were glad to find ourselves on level

B

ground and to be allowed to take our seats in the "Einspänner." After Ettal there is no more ascent ; a level road, bordered on either side by mountain ash, soon brought us to our long wished-for goal. We had telegraphed to Frau Mayr the day before, asking her either to receive us or find rooms for us ; so we drove straight to the house of "the Christus," and were met at the door by his genial wife. She accepted us at once as friends, for the sake of friends of ours who had made a long stay at her house, but explained that she could not receive us, as their rooms were engaged for the Duke and Duchess of Connaught. While we were speaking to her, the well-known face of the Christus appeared in the doorway, his splendid long black ringlets hanging on his shoulders. He doffed his cap, greeted us courteously, and told us that they had taken a "fair chamber" for us at Johann Rutz's, "King Herod's" house, and their eldest girl, a sweet little maid of about ten, got up beside our driver to guide him through the puzzling labyrinth of the village. Our restingplace was close to the church, standing like all the houses in its own garden. We were met at the gate by a beautiful boy of sixteen, a quantity of close curling fair hair making a kind of halo round a face full of earnest pathetic expression. This was Wilhelm, "Herod's" eldest boy ; he does not look more than thirteen, but all the attendance on his father's guests seemed to fall on his shoulders. I asked him what part he took in the Play. "Joseph sold by his brethren," was the reply.

He began busily to unfasten our packages, while we were handed over to the kind and motherly Frau Rutz. She led us up a ladder-like staircase to our room, which was exquisitely clean. The whole furniture consisted of two beds, two tables, two chairs, and a few pegs on a stand with a curtain in front.

The house was very quiet, as was the village, for hardly any visitors arrive until Friday, and most not till Saturday. We went down to the sitting-room of the family, opening from the shop (Herod is the baker of the village), and found a roast hen provided for our supper. Presently our host came in, and after saluting us, sat down quite simply at another table, where he was joined by his wife, his daughter, and "Joseph," and they took their simple supper of cups of soup with bread in it.

Next morning the church bells began about four, and rang at intervals till eight, when High Mass began. I was too tired to go, but the music sounded beautiful as it came wafted in from the open church door. M——, who went to the Hoch-Amt, told me that all was most reverently done, and the congregation most devout ; the music she thought wonderful for a village choir, especially the execution of a chorale of Bach.

Our little valet, "Joseph," as we could not help calling him, brought our breakfast upstairs ; when we went down to the sitting-room we found Herod and Barabbas sitting at one table over some papers, a maid ironing at another, and Joseph washing his face and neck in a corner. There is a handsome old bureau in the room, which Rutz told me he had bought from a priest, and Joseph's guitar hangs on the wall; the rest of the furniture consists of the usual huge green earthenware stove, two long tables with benches, a large wooden wardrobe, which seemed to contain the family linen, and a kind of settle sofa, which I suspect was Joseph's resting-place at night.

The rain was almost incessant, but we paddled out through seas of mud. Frau Mayr had charged us to return and pay her a visit, and on our arrival she received us affectionately, and begged us to come and look at the rooms she was preparing for our Prince and Princess, his " Hof-Marschall," as she called him, and his wife. She has a lovely little girl of about four, who flew at my watch and châtelaine, chattering and pulling them about in spite of her mother's reproofs.

We then went to the house of Peter (Jacob Hett), having heard that he was one of the best carvers in the village; he told us he carved nothing but crucifixes. He was very pleasant, talking simply about his part in the Play. I asked him how he had studied it; whether he had followed his predecessor's line. He answered very emphatically, " Nein, er hat nicht gut gespielt."*

We were anxious to call upon the Geistlicher Rath Daisenberger; Hett assured us he would welcome us, and took us to his house. It was with true reverence and respect that we entered that humble dwelling. For thirty years Daisenberger was not only parish priest of Ober-Ammergau, but the director of the Passion Play, remodelling, rewriting, training his peasant flock; in a word, the soul of the whole thing.

The result, the whole atmosphere of the village and *morale* of the people, as well as the artistic excellence of their performance, tell us what the man must be who for more than a generation has been their intellectual leader, as well as all that is expressed in " Seelsorger," that tender word which it is impossible to translate. He is now eighty-two, and has retired from his charge, with the honorary title, bestowed on him by the King, of Geistlicher Rath.

He wrote several plays for the instruction and exercise in acting of his people, amongst others a translation of the " Antigone "; and we wished to find out whether we could procure any of them. His two maid-servants were busy on the ground-floor, and bade us go upstairs. On the little landing was a bookcase filled with Greek and Latin classics, and in a room as simple as a peasant's we found the venerable old man. He received us most kindly, insisting on rising from his chair, although infirm. He was sitting at a table with a few books before him, and a little pile in a window-seat at hand; amongst others, New Testaments in different languages. He made very little of his dramas, said they were all in manuscript, but lent me a German New Testament, which I had been told would be useful at the Play.

We then went to the house of Gregor Lechner (Judas), and found

---

* " No, he did not act well."

him sitting on his little bench carving. He impressed and attracted me more than any of the peasants whom we have seen; there is something of genius and poetry in his face, and he is exquisitely refined and gentle in manner. All the villagers with whom we have made acquaintance are refined, through the good breeding of simplicity and kindly feeling; but there is something more in the conversation of Lechner; a beautiful and gifted soul looks through his eyes, and speaks in every tone of his voice.

We bought a few photographs, among them one of our host, and returned to find him hard at work in his baker's shop. He laughed when we showed him our purchase; certainly he looked rather different, in his worn jacket and carpet slippers, from the splendidly attired monarch. But it is a good face. Few of the men of Ober-Ammergau have good figures, their legs being generally too short in proportion to the body; but this is much concealed by their robes on the stage. There is little beauty amongst the women, but the children are almost all pretty; they mostly go bare-foot. If asked what part they take in the Play, the answer is generally, "ein Engel," or "Adam's Kind," or "beim Volk," *i.e.* amongst the multitude in the first scene.

We were early in church next morning. There was no High Mass; but the number of celebrations seemed endless, and we were told the sacristy was full of priests waiting to say their Mass. There were five altars, and these were continually occupied for several hours. One of the last to celebrate was the venerable Daisenberger, who, in spite of his infirmities, comes every morning to church, winter and summer, to say Mass.

The rain was incessant all Saturday. In the evening we went out to see the crowds come in, but the slush underneath, and misty rain overhead, sadly marred all that would otherwise have worn a festal aspect. In spite of the weather the throng was great, and the stream of vehicles of all kinds seemed endless, from smart carriages to long covered carts, drawn by bullocks and filled with peasants. Amongst the former, one carriage passed us with two such tidy little portmanteaus strapped outside, that we at once decided it must belong to our English Prince and Princess; and so it proved, for very soon the tall and striking figure of the Christus appeared, escorting his royal guests, who walked in Irish fashion, he in front, and she picking her steps with little gaitered feet through the mud. Indeed, it was impossible for two people to keep side by side in those seas of trodden slush; every one was obliged to shift for himself.

There was no sleep possible on Sunday morning after four o'clock. Frau Rutz told me she had been up at three, and Joseph also; they had been to the four o'clock service, where Joseph and his little brother of ten had communicated, in common with almost all the actors. When we went into the church at a quarter before six it was so crowded at the door that I thought we could not get a seat; however, on going higher up we

PLAN OF THE THEATRE AT OBER-AMMERGAU

IN 1880.

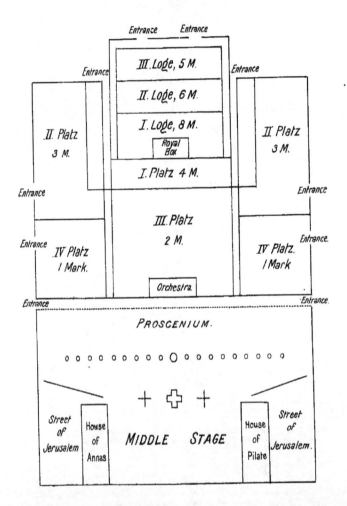

The 19 spots marked on the Proscenium show the places of the Chorus, with the leader in the middle. The two lines at an angle show their position when they moved to either side during the Tableaux. The three crosses on the middle stage mark the spot where the Crucifixion was represented. The seats of the I, II, and III "Loge" as well as those of the I and II "Platz" were covered.

BRETTELL, 51, RUPERT ST. LONDON, W.

found a clear space in the aisle. There was a High Celebration; and we returned to breakfast, in the arbour in our garden, before seven. For the rain and mist had cleared away, the heavy bank of clouds was lifted from the mountains, and for the first time we saw the peaks and slopes of the hills bright with sunshine.

Alas! we had no tickets for the theatre. It had been impossible to fix our time of arriving until the very day before we came, and Mayr told us at once that every ticket for the reserved covered seats for Sunday was gone; but that we should have the best places on Monday.

However, we joined the stream of people who flocked to the theatre in a meadow at the other end of the village from the church, and on arriving peeped through the open doors at the great area and tiers of seats, already apparently filling to overflowing. I ran up a flight of stairs leading to the lower covered seats, and through the door could just see, as the gun was fired, a rainbow-clad band of crowned noble-looking beings appear upon the stage. Then the door was inexorably closed, and we were mournfully turning away, when two tickets for unreserved places were offered to us. Mine was for the cheapest place of all, amongst the peasants, nearest the stage. I thankfully accepted it, and in a few moments found myself inside the theatre, where on a side bench room was just made for one.

In attempting to write my impressions of the most wonderful thing I ever saw, I ought to say that they are the result of two days spent in the theatre; for on Monday we received tickets for the "logen," and again witnessed the whole of the Passions-Spiel. The second time I took notes during almost the whole time; I had taken none the first day.

Far from the impression received being weakened by repetition, it was much greater and more intense the second time than the first. I think this may partly be because the first time it is seen we feel more of curiosity and surprise than the second time, when the mind is in a more passive state for receiving impressions, and responding harmoniously to the wonderful influence of scenes, words, and music.

The first sight of the Chorus is something which can never be forgotten—the band of peasants, fresh from their daily work, every expression, every movement and action of the limbs full of dignity, grace and beauty, of noble simplicity, and entire absence of self-consciousness. I was, as I have said, the nearest to them of any in the theatre, so that I could see every movement and play of feature perfectly clearly. But no distance was needed to lend enchantment to those noble figures and faces; they never failed to charm and to win respect. There are eighteen in the Chorus, eight men and ten women; the Choragus, who speaks the prologues, standing in the centre of the proscenium, with four men on the

right and three on the left, while five female figures stand on either side
of the men. Their robes and the blending of colour are alone striking
and beautiful ; all alike wear a long white under-tunic edged with gold
round the neck and skirt, with a coloured outer mantle edged with the
Greek key pattern in gold, and held together by a band across the breast ;
a girdle round the white under robe, of the colour of the mantle mixed
with gold ; sandals on the feet, with two straps across the instep over hose
of the colour of the mantle ; on the head a golden diadem with a cross in
the floriated centre.

These robes form a brilliant but harmonious chord of colour. The
Choragus is conspicuous by his scarlet mantle ; next to him on the right
is green, then a brownish-red, green again, and purple ; the five women
wear a bright sort of magenta, purple, dark blue, brown-red, and light
blue. The three men to the left of the Choragus wear green, dark
red, and purple ; the women magenta, purple, a bright grey, reddish-
brown, and light blue.

I do not think that sufficient prominence has been given to the part
sustained by this admirable Chorus in most of the descriptions of the
"Passions-Spiel," and I have even heard spectators say that they were
slightly wearied by it ; but to me they were throughout true "Schutz-
Geister," as they are called, keeping the soul in tune and assisting it
most truly in the long effort of mind and heart which the tremendous
drama requires.

The Choragus greets all who have come together in sympathetic
words, accepting them at once as friends who are like-minded with the
performers, and exhorting them to assist devoutly at the Mystery to be
set forth, which is nothing less than the redemption of the world. "All
hail ! welcome to the band of brothers, whom love divine hath here
assembled, who wish to share the sorrows of their Saviour, and to follow
Him, step by step, on the way of His sufferings to the Cross and the
Sepulchre." The key-note to the whole is given in this first solemnly
intoned prologue :—

> "Ich will"—so spricht der Herr—
> "Den Tod des Sünders nicht,"*

and is sustained in the lines sung as the Chorus divide and retire to either
side of the stage ; while the curtain rises, and we see the first typical
tableau from the Old Testament, Adam and Eve driven from Paradise.

> "Doch von Ferne, von Calvaria's Höhen,
> Leuchtet durch die Nacht ein Morgenglüh'n,"†

is sweetly intoned by the Choragus. From this moment the "Schutz-
Geister" become, as it were, our spiritual guides, and we have but to

---

* "I desire not the death of a sinner, saith the Lord."
† "Yet from afar, from Calvary's height, shines through the night the morning-dawn."

surrender ourselves to their teaching and to the impressions of the scenes set forth.

The first tableau, the Expulsion from Paradise, seemed to me, artistically, amongst the least successful, partly because the eye was worried by the contrast between the upper limbs and shoulder of the chief figure, Adam, which were bare, and the lower, which, with the feet, were clothed in " tricot "; the effect, at least from very near, was not good, and, as there is abundant drapery of skins, it seems quite needless. Besides this, the angels are throughout unsuccessful, although less so in a tableau than in action.

But nothing can be more lovely than the second tableau, which follows in a few minutes. The curtain has fallen on the scene of the Expulsion, the Chorus has formed again in a straight line, continuing the song of thanksgiving for redemption ; and now, as they retire, the curtain rises, and we behold the Tree of Life, the Cross, on a rocky mount. At its foot kneels a girl of about thirteen, clasping it in her arms ; while twelve children, clad as angels, are grouped around in attitudes of adoring thanksgiving. The grace and beauty of this picture are wonderful, and also the motionless acting of the infants, many of them with outstretched arms. Amongst them was a flaxen-haired babe of about two, kneeling with clasped hands, while an elder girl laid one hand on its shoulder, and with the other pointed to the Cross. During this tableau alone the " Schutz-Geister," having, as usual, retired to the sides of the stage, kneel while they sing :—

"Ew'ger, höre deiner Kinder Stammeln," &c. ;*

and then again exhort the spectators

"Folget dem Versöhner nun zu Seite."†

Now the first scene in the "Passions-Spiel" begins. Often as we had read and heard of the Entry into Jerusalem acted in that theatre, the reality far exceeded our expectations, at least *before* the central figure actually appeared. It was to me one of the most moving, and quite overcoming, scenes in the whole drama, as the seemingly endless crowd flowed on, men, women, and children all swayed by one sentiment, every voice joining in the—

Heil Dir, Heil Dir, O Da - vid's Sohn! Heil, etc.

There is much dignity in the conception of this march chorale : it is one

---

* " Eternal, hear thy children's prayer."
† " Follow the Redeemer now beside."

of the most successful pieces in the " Passions-Musik." But of course the opportunity is a grand one for a musician : the distance in which it is first softly heard, the waving accompaniment of arms and green branches, the onward procession. The change in the spirit of the words for a while from praise to prayer is plaintively illustrated by the music while the surging crowd advances, their voices growing louder and the air more defined. It is an affecting appeal written from the heart, and powerful to make the listener one in sympathy with the unanimous throng. I give the music of the second verse.

The "Volk," as they say, come slowly on, waving branches of bracken, the action of the arms and of the limbs full of indescribable grace, although those in front are half-backing, as in royal presence. We feel that every eye is fixed upon One whom as yet we do not see, and that the multitude have but one soul, filled with adoring homage to Him, "Der in des Höchsten Namen kommt." Old words, old visions of childhood return to the heart: the great multitude which no man may number, with palms in their hands ; the everlasting song of blessing, and honour, and glory, and power to the Prince of the kings of the earth ; and we seem to see a faint shadow of that which shall be when every discordant note has ceased, and the soul is set free for the endless harmony of thanksgiving.

Shall I acknowledge that the first appearance of the Christus was a disappointment? perhaps because expectation had been wound too high by the song and triumph of the multitude. At all events, the first strong feeling was, " he has attempted the *impossible.*" The attitude, sitting sideways on the ass, also, I think, takes off from the effect; and the first words he utters, not being in Holy Scripture, increase the feeling of strangeness and disappointment, "Was sehe ich hier? Ist das Gottes Haus, oder ist es ein Marktplatz?"* he exclaims in accents of strong indignation. But throughout the scene, the only one in which he uses energetic action, he is perfectly dignified, and his last words, "Kommt, mein Jünger, ich habe gethan, was der Vater mich geheissen hat,"† give us the *motif* which is so admirably worked out by Mayr. His conception in that respect of one "driven by the Spirit" seems to me beyond praise. "Lo! I come to do Thy Will" is expressed in every word and action, bringing the thought before the spectators with marvellous vividness. He is possessed by his mission, and throughout the tumult and variety of the "Spiel" this calm unity of unwavering purpose is expressed with unfailing force.

Mayr's voice is by far the clearest and easiest to follow amongst the actors. The German New Testament with which the "Geistlicher Rath" had provided me was needless, the familiar words were so clearly spoken; and those sentences in his part which were not from Holy Scripture were also quite distinct. In common with the other actors he had some peculiarities of pronunciation; for instance, "dich" and "doch" were pronounced "*disch*" and "*dosch.*" Many of the actors spoke most indistinctly, and, having only the text of the choruses and prologues in our handbooks, we were dependent on the speakers for knowledge of the dialogue of the drama.

To judge by pictures and by his present appearance, the face of Tobias Flunger, the Christus of 1850, must have suited his part better than that of Mayr, which is too short in proportion to its breadth. The face is best when seen in profile, and when the head is somewhat raised, as in speaking; when he ceases to speak, his head sinks on his breast with a slight circular sweep towards the right, which has a certain mannerism in it, and is, I think, less dignified and simple than a perfectly straight inclination would be.

The anger of the traders whom Christ has driven from the Temple, and the zeal of the priests to use it for their own ends, are finely brought out, and the first appearance of the Sanhedrim (prefaced by the tableau of the conspiracy of Joseph's brethren) is most striking and splendid; in the colouring a wonderful use is made of blue and purple robes.

Caiaphas now appears in his white robes‡ (the Bürgermeister, Johann Lang), and henceforth becomes the principal *actor* in the drama. The

---

* "What do I behold? Is this God's House? or is it a market-place?"
† "Come, my disciples, I have done what the Father commanded me to do."
‡ The robes of Annas are of cloth of gold, with a gold horned mitre on his head; while Caiaphas is in white, even to his shoes, embroidered with gold. Nathanael, his chief helper, and bitter enemy of Christ, wears red, with a blue mitre.

chief burden of the action and *entrain* rests upon him ; nothing would be accomplished but for his deep-seated and untiring efforts to compass the destruction of the Prophet Who has won the Hosannas of the multitude. In speaking of the different actors, the venerable Daisenberger seemed anxious that the merit of Lang's acting should be recognized. He told me that he thought it one of the most difficult parts ; I think he said *the* most difficult.

In this first council every consideration is urged which could inflame the audience—zeal for the law of Moses, fear of the Romans, fear for their own safety, lest Christ should stir up the people against them, and so " we should take the place which we have prepared for Him."

To the traders who are brought in, and who bitterly complain of their losses, compensation is promised from the Temple treasury, and their right of trading in the courts of the Temple, granted by the High Priest, is reaffirmed. Still, "fear of the people" prevails ; the Prophet must be taken secretly and at night, and full power is given to the chief trader (Dathan), who thinks he can do something with Judas, to offer any bribe in the name of the Council.

We are, of course, accustomed to dwell chiefly on the supernatural causes for His Passion Who was delivered by the determinate counsel and foreknowledge of God ; but the leading thought in the construction of the Ammergau play is the human passions by which the Divine Counsel was worked out ; the *natural* causes, if we may so say, for the condemnation and death, on Friday, of Him Who on Sunday entered Jerusalem in triumph.

The effect on the priests of the raising of Lazarus cannot be brought in, because it lies too far behind the moment when the action of the play begins. But we are shown that three causes worked together for the destruction of the Messiah—the intense resentment of the traders at His interference with their gainful traffic, and their desire for revenge ; the anger of the High Priest at the authority assumed by our Lord in the Temple ; and the avarice and selfish fears of Judas. These are woven with true art into a threefold thread, which runs through the whole story, gradually unfolding the natural causes for the rapid and tremendous change between the "Einzug" and the "Kreuzweg." It is remarkable how Caiaphas endeavours to inflame the passions which, both in the traders and in Judas, are working for his purposes, while the traders, on their part, appeal to the jealousy of the priests for their own authority : "Hath not the Hohe Rath given us leave to set out for sale openly in the courts of the Temple all that is necessary for sacrifice ?"

The parting of Tobias from his parents is a beautiful tableau, and lasted for three minutes, while in solo and chorus was sung—

"Ach sie kommt die Scheidestunde, &c."

The Chorus enlarge on the sorrows of a mother's heart :—

" Bis ein sel'ger Augenblick
In den Mutterschooss zurück
Den geliebten Sohn wird führen."*

The second tableau, the Lamenting Bride of the Canticles, was amongst the least interesting, although it is evidently got up with much care, and seems a favourite with the peasants. The music of the Bride's Lament, sung by one female soprano voice, is the most ambitious in the Passion Play, and certainly overtaxed the powers of the vocalist.

Christ and the twelve Apostles now appear on the scene, and the question asked of our Lord after His Resurrection, " Lord, wilt thou at this time restore again the kingdom to Israel?" is here put into Philip's mouth. Christ answers him nearly in the words of St. Luke xviii. 32, 33, " The Son of man must be delivered to the Gentiles," &c., and answers further questions in words from St. John xii. 23, 24, 32, and 35.

Simon, with the family from Bethany, meets Him, and Christ accepts the invitation to Simon's house. "Conqueror of Death!" Lazarus exclaims; Mary Magdalene asks Him if He will accept a token of love from her; and Martha entreats to be allowed to serve Him. "Do, pious souls, that which you have purposed to do," He answers, and blesses them. The peaceful scene of the supper at Simon's house contrasts finely with the tumultuous action of the greater part of the play. It was one of those which brought more vividly than anything ever previously had done before the mind, how He, Perfect Man, had lived and gone in and out amongst men as their familiar friend and companion. "Jerusalem!" He says, "O that my coming were as welcome to thee as it is to these my friends!" When Mary pours the ointment on His feet, the Christus, raising His hand, says the one word, "Maria!" in the tone of one touched to the heart.

The wonderful acting of Judas now becomes prominent—the dialogue between him and the Christus being lengthened from the Scripture account. "What a waste!" Judas says with vexation. "Friend Judas, look me in the face. Waste on Me—thy Master?" The concluding words, "Wheresoever this Gospel shall be preached in the whole world," &c., are inexpressibly touching, as we actually behold their fulfilment after nearly twenty centuries in a remote Bavarian village.

In "The Parting at Bethany," which followed, Mayr's acting was most admirable. "Once more, farewell, beloved, peaceful Bethany! never more shall I tarry amid thy still valleys." And in the scene with His Mother he sustains his part with true feeling and dignity. Most instructive is the human tenderness, undiminished by overpowering sense of a mission to be fulfilled which must bring agony to her He would fain spare. Every movement in this scene is tender and graceful, especially

* " Till a blessed time of meeting
To his mother's arms once more
Shall restore her darling son."

the clinging clasp of the hand even after He has parted from His Mother's embrace and turned to leave her. The words he speaks are, like all, distinctly uttered: "Thou wilt suffer with me, dearest Mother, wilt battle with me in my mortal struggle, and also take part in my triumph." The whole dialogue, none of it of course from Holy Writ, is in the highest tone of resignation and mutual love. His thanks to Mary were especially touching; contrasting, alas! with the thanklessness with which a mother's devotion is too often received, as though it were a thing of course. "Mother, Mother, for the tender love and Motherly care which thou hast shown to me during the three-and-thirty years of my life, receive the tender gratitude of thy Son." And nothing can be more perfect than His last words, as He gives her into Simon's care, in answer to her question, "Where shall I see thee again?" "There, beloved Mother, where the Scripture shall be fulfilled: as a lamb brought to the slaughter, so He openeth not His mouth."

The fourth act begins with the tableau, containing thirty-seven figures, of the rejection of Vashti, and espousal of Esther. The Choragus presses home the lesson, and before the curtain rises the Chorus sing :—

"Jerusalem! Jerusalem! erwache!
Erkenne was zum Frieden dir noch werden kann."*

This is one of the most striking pieces in the music: it is introduced by a bass voice, and taken up by the Chorus.

In the scene which follows, of the weeping over Jerusalem, the Christus, in answer to the appeal of the disciples to establish the Kingdom of God upon earth, again refers all to the Father's Will: "Children, what ye desire will come to pass in its own time. But my ways are prepared for me of my Father; and thus saith the Lord: My thoughts are not your thoughts, and your ways are not my ways." He sends Peter and John to prepare the Passover, and they kneel and ask His blessing. A fine piece of acting on Judas' part follows, as he shows his empty bag to the Master, disregards His assurance that they need not be careful, and says, "If only the worth of that ointment were therein! Three hundred pieces of silver! How long we might then have lived without anxiety!" He remains behind when the rest of the disciples follow their Master to the Temple, and his soliloquy betrays the disposition of mind which made him an easy prey. He complains of his Master's prophecies of coming trouble: "I am weary of believing and hoping. There is nothing before us but poverty and low estate. . . . I will turn back. Happily I have been provident, and from time to time have laid aside a little out of the bag in case of need. If only that fool had put the worth of her oint-ment into the bag, it would have fallen into my hands, now that it seems

* "Jerusalem! Jerusalem! awake!
And know the peace which still may be thine own."

likely that our brotherhood will be dissolved. As it is, I must look out for some means of support."

From this time Judas becomes evidently the person who arouses the greatest interest among the peasant audience. Being amongst them, I could hear their remarks and watch their ways. It must be acknowledged that they were considerably on the look-out for anything, however grimly, amusing. One could imagine the delight they must have taken in the grotesque parts of the old play, and their keen interest in the actual hanging of Judas, surrounded by imps gobbling up the sausages which represented the entrails of the traitor.

As it is, in spite of the grave and severe treatment of the terrible tragedy in the present version, the peasants seemed to me quick to seize on the grotesque element wherever it was possible throughout the performance. I do not speak of the Ammergauers; those around me were chiefly peasants from a distance who had come to see the play, and who, though perfectly orderly and reverent, certainly possessed that desire to be amused in the midst of most solemn tragedy, for the satisfaction of which largest provision was made in mediæval Scripture plays.

All the following scene, when Judas is persuaded by the scourged traders to betray his Master, was followed with deep interest, and they seemed to listen breathlessly to his monologue when left alone, in which he weighs the probabilities of success, considering in all things the effect of circumstances on his own interests. If the priests succeed he will become a famous man, as having helped to save the law of Moses; should the Master conquer "I will cast myself repentant at His feet. He is really good; never have I seen Him repulse a penitent."

Lechner's acting and intonation in this scene can never be forgotten, especially when the thought of meeting his Master's glance nearly overwhelms him. "I shall not be able to bear His piercing gaze," he cries out, already seeming to feel the gnawing of endless remorse for the crime not yet consummated. "My companions will see in my face that I am a —— No! I will not be that—I am no traitor! I do nothing but show the Jews where the Master may be: treachery means more than that."

The grouping of the first tableau which precedes the fifth act, the Manna in the Wilderness, is quite marvellous: I counted seventy-eight figures. One of the most surprising things was the extreme rapidity with which, after the curtain fell, a second tableau, of the Grapes from Canaan, was formed.

In the next scene, the Last Supper, the words are almost entirely from Holy Scripture; the account in St. Luke of strife for precedence among the disciples being woven into the narrative of St. John. The whole of our Lord's reproof in St. Luke xxii. is given, though not exactly in the same order, but thus: verses 28, 29, 30, 25, 26, and 27. At the last words, "I am among you as he that serveth," the Christus rises,

and, laying aside His upper garment, girded with a towel, He says to
Peter, "Petrus, gib mir deinen Fuss." The rest of the dialogue exactly
follows St. John's account, as also the words spoken when He has sat
down. He rises for the Institution of the Eucharist, and says, "The old
Covenant, which my Father made with Abraham, Isaac, and Jacob, has
reached its close. And I say unto you, A new Covenant is beginning,
which I solemnly consecrate to-day in my blood, as the Father hath
delivered to me, and it will last till all shall be fulfilled." The actual
words of consecration followed. Mayr's acting and movements throughout this scene, which demanded so much, were perfect and solemn : there
was a marvellous effect in the raising of the hands and laying them upon
the bread, as though Divinity were poured out in action. All that follows
is admirable : the administration—the action and expression of Judas in
receiving—the bearing of all the Apostles. After the reception, the
Christus says : "My children, abide in me, and I in you. As the Father
hath loved me, so have I loved you : continue ye in my love." And
then, after the prophecy of the betrayal by Judas, and the denial of
Peter, part of the discourse in St. John xiv. follows ; the feeling and
intonation with which Mayr gives it being most harmonious and
beautiful.

He comes forward to the front of the stage, and raising his eyes to
heaven recites a hymn of thanksgiving (Psalm cxvii.); then, looking
lovingly on his sorrowful companions, says in accents of solemn tenderness : "My children, why are ye so sad, and why do ye gaze on me so
mournfully ? Let not your heart be troubled ; ye believe in God, believe
also in Me. In my Father's house are many mansions." And the solemn
words are continued in tones of such affecting devoutness that we grieve
when they are ended.

There is a certain relief to the strain of mind and feeling which the
scenes involve, in the tableaux and songs of the Chorus, while yet the
latter never fail to bring home to the conscience the lesson of what we
behold. The sixth act begins with the tableau of Joseph sold by his
Brethren, while the Chorus sings :—

Was   bie - tet   für   den   Kna   ben   ihr?

"So sprechen, Brüder, wenn euch wir
    Ihn kauflich übergeben ?"*

* "What will ye offer for the lad ?—
    Answer us, brothers,—if we now
    For gold deliver him to you ?"

And then they remind us:—

> " Wie oft habt ihr durch eure Thaten
> Auch euren Gott verkauft—verrathen ! "*

The contrast is tremendous between the scene which follows, Judas before the Sanhedrim, and the closing scene of the preceding act. For acting and force it was one of the most striking in the play, and perhaps Lechner's acting was at its best here. The mixture of irresolution and determination, of lingering regrets and eagerness to grasp the reward just within his reach, was perfectly expressed. He cannot bear to be questioned as to the cause of his rupture with his Master, answers Caiaphas surlily, and after the fearful words, which are the sad story of many a soul, " The friendship between him and me has for some time become cooler," breaks out abruptly with the question, " What will ye *give* me if I deliver Him unto you ? "

I do not believe any mere reading of the narrative could bring the awful tragedy of such a choice before some minds as Lechner's acting does—the choice which each soul must make between the dust of earth and the treasures of eternity. It is brought out also with great skill and terrible irony in the text. "Only think, Judas," Dathan says; "thirty pieces of silver! What a prize!" Then he is flattered, told that much more will be done for him, that he will become a man of mark and distinction, till the last wavering of the will is overcome, and he cries out, "I am content!" and then aside, "My fortune is made!" This single moment of fearful contentment and elation is his; in the very next he cowers before the indignant outburst of reproach addressed to him by Nicodemus.

The eagerness with which he claws each piece of silver as it is reckoned to him, and drops it into his bag, has often been described. He was last seen at the table of his Lord—now he is taking counsel with His enemies, has come into their secret, and united himself to the assembly gathered together against the soul of the righteous. And with overpowering horror the words of the Chorus ring in our ears:—

> " Was diese Scene uns vorhält,
> Ist ein getreues Bild der Welt."†

When Judas has left the council, Caiaphas becomes the chief actor: his iron will treads out any spark of opposition kindled by Nicodemus and Joseph of Arimathea, who leave the council after a vehement protest. Hitherto only bonds and imprisonment have been spoken of for the

* " How oft have ye through evil deeds
   Your God even thus betrayed and sold !"

† " A faithful picture of the world
   In this sad scene before us lies."

Prophet; now Caiaphas with splendid action pronounces his decision: "Hearken to your High Priest! It is better that one man die for the people, and that the whole nation perish not. HE MUST DIE! No peace in Israel without His death!" "God has spoken through His High Priest," a Rabbi exclaims; "only through His death can the people of Israel be saved." The council breaks up without any solemn blessing from the High Priest, but with a tumultuous outcry of, "Let Him die, the enemy of our holy law!" So ends this wonderful scene, the counterpart to the intense calm of the one which preceded it, the closing words of which still echo in the heart: "But that the world may know that I love the Father, and as the Father hath given me commandment, even so I do."

A beautiful tableau introduces the seventh act: Adam tilling the ground, with his children around him, while Eve sits a little apart—a babe in her lap and a little one by her knee—eleven children in all. Here again the effect is rather marred by the contrast between the glaring "tricot" worn by Eve and the lovely bare limbs of the children. There is a second tableau, in which twenty-four take part, of Joab treacherously slaying Amasa, which lasted for quite three minutes.

The Agony in the Garden must be one of the most difficult pieces of acting in Mayr's part; but he brings to it intense feeling, devotion, and dignity. Never can the tone be forgotten in which he exclaims, as from the depth of a broken heart, "Vater!—Mein Vater!" or the touching tenderness of his complaint when he returns for the second time to the sleeping Apostles: "O my most trusted ones! Even amongst you I find none to comfort me." The anguish becomes keener and more fearful in its expression: "The sorrows of death encompass me. . . . O sin! O sins of mankind, ye weigh me down! O fearful burden! My Father! . . . Thy most holy will! Father! Thy Son! hear Him!" Then, as the Christus "reels in the victorious fight," an angel appears. It were better, I think, if no words were spoken, and if the angel were only to support the head which leans on the arms of the messenger in mortal exhaustion. When He speaks once more, He has been strengthened. "Yea, holy Father! . . . I will accomplish it! . . . Reconciliation, salvation, blessedness!"

There were moments like these, during the play, when the thought forced itself on one's mind: "These are the people to whom some amongst us would fain 'preach the Gospel.'" No one could have acted, I suppose, as Mayr did—certainly not a peasant wood-carver—who was not penetrated by the awful truths which he set forth. And he is but the representative of that which has for hundreds of years flourished in his village, and which finds expression in the text of the Passion Play.

The taking of the Christus by the soldiers of the High Priest ends the first part of the "*Passions-Drama.*"

We had but time for a hurried meal at Frau Rutz', and then drove back to the theatre about half an hour before the second part began; for, not having reserved places, we were anxious to have a good choice among the unreserved ones. Just as we reached the theatre, rain began to fall rather heavily, and the orchestra was moved from the centre, close to the stage, to the side near the lowest door, where there was an awning. Their former station was therefore left free, and benches were moved into it for spectators. Close to this area I found a seat on the front bench of all, which fortunately had a back, so that I was as close to the stage as it was possible to be. Until one o'clock, when the second part of the play began, the theatre was filled by a forest of umbrellas; a peasant woman next to me gave me a share of hers, and told me how she had come with her husband from a distant village to see the "Passions-Spiel" for the first time.

The rain had not ceased when the gun was fired, and the Chorus appeared on the stage; but every umbrella was put down, and we covered ourselves with cloaks as best we could. Happily, it was not cold, and soon the sun shone out, the rain ceased, and the rest of the afternoon was most lovely; indeed, I believe those to the right in the theatre suffered from the heat of the western sun. On the left we were in shade.

The first tableau, containing thirty figures, of Zedekiah smiting Micaiah on the cheek, precedes the scene of our Lord before Annas. The conception of the character of Annas is of one even more filled than Caiaphas with thirst for the blood of the Christ; though, from his age, with less power to carry his designs into action, and suffering from the restless desire to see them accomplished.

He appears with his friends on the balcony of his house, saying that he cannot rest that night until he knows that the disturber of peace is in bonds, &c. The priests try to pacify him, telling him that the prisoner will soon be here. When the Christus is led in, the Scripture narrative is followed, and the mournful leading about from one tribunal to another begins. Mocked by the soldiers, He is led to Caiaphas, who holds his court in the middle of the stage. Two tableaux, the stoning of Naboth, and Job, preceded this scene, the latter not successfully conceived or carried out; but the chorus sung during its exhibition was particularly striking and touching, with its continual *refrain* of "Ach! welch ein Mensch!"

Here, again, I am sure that to some minds old truths were brought home more deeply than they had ever been before. The chorus, the tableau, and the following scenes were the setting forth visibly of the old words: "As for me, I am a worm and no man."

C

"Ach ! welch ein Mensch !
O alle ihr gerührten Herzen !
Ach ! Jesus, Jesus ! Gottes Sohn,
Wird loser Knechte Spott und Hohn
Bei endelosem Kampf der Schmerzen.
Ach ! welch ein Mensch !"*

"How," we could not but ask ourselves, "have these peasant artists learned, both in action and in the long choruses which are interwoven with the scenes, to instruct those who have had every opportunity for instruction and reflection on the subject-matter of their drama, and to impress, as they never before were impressed, the very people who have meditated most deeply on the narrative of the Passion ?"

The intense aggravation which must have been caused to the sufferings of One already exhausted in body and mind, by the repeated dragging about from tribunal to tribunal, would probably be brought home for the first time to the hearts of many by the action of the "Passions-Spiel." The mockery of the guards, as they lead the Christus from one to another, does but fill in the scenes which we feel sure, from the narrative of the Gospels, must have taken place.

The trial before Caiaphas is chiefly an expansion of the scene described by St. Matthew in four words : "many false witnesses came." One after another steps forward, confronting the silent Prisoner, who stands motionless ; the cord which binds His hands behind His back held by one of the mocking guard. In 1860 Mayr personated Balbus, the servant of Annas, who strikes Christ on the cheek, and who continues to mock Him on the way to Caiaphas, and during the trial.'

The false witnesses declare that the Christ has forbidden to pay tribute to Cæsar ; that, in spite of the law, He has sat down at table without washing His hands ; that He has had friendly intercourse with publicans and sinners, and even gone to their houses and eaten with them ; that they have heard from trustworthy folk that He spoke to Samaritans, and spent a whole day with them ; that on the Sabbath He healed the sick, and ordered a man to carry his bed on the Sabbath day ; and one declares, "Thou didst presume—I was present—to forgive sins, which belongs only to God." "Thou hast also blasphemed God," another breaks in, "and dared to say that Thou wast One with the Father." Finally, two witness against Him, as recorded in the Gospels ; and Caiaphas, having many times during the accusations in vain questioned his Prisoner, rises, and with grand action says, "Thou thinkest to save Thyself by silence ; Thou darest not to acknowledge, before the Fathers

* "Alas ! Behold the man !
O all ye tender-hearted souls.
Ah, Jesu, Jesu, Son of God,
Becomes the scorn and jest of knaves,
Amidst His awful strife with pain.
Alas ! Behold the Man !"

of the people, what Thou hast taught to the people. Or darest Thou?
Then hearken: I, the High Priest, adjure Thee by the living God!
Speak, art Thou the Messiah, the Son of the most high God?"

Then the long silence of the Christus is broken: "Thou sayest that
I am. Nevertheless I say unto you, Hereafter ye shall see the Son of man
sitting on the right hand of power, and coming in the clouds of heaven."
Caiaphas tears asunder his upper garment, with horror on his countenance,
exclaiming, "He has blasphemed God. . . . But not I, not the Council—
the law of God itself dooms Him to death." He then appeals to the
scribes, to read publicly the sentence, in the law of Moses, on him who
rebels against rulers ordained of God ; and a scribe reads from a roll:
"The man that will do presumptuously, and will not hearken unto the
priest that standeth to minister there before the Lord thy God, or unto
the judge, even that man shall die: and thou shalt put away the evil
from Israel."*

Another, at the command of Caiaphas, reads the sentence on the
Sabbath-breaker: "Ye shall keep the Sabbath therefore; for it is holy
unto you: every one that defileth it shall surely be put to death: for
whosoever doeth any work therein, that soul shall be cut off from among
his people."†

Caiaphas then demands: "How doth the law punish a blasphemer?"
And a third priest reads: "Speak unto the children of Israel, saying,
Whosoever curseth his God shall bear his sin. And he that blasphemeth
the name of the Lord, he shall surely be put to death ; all the congregation shall certainly stone him, as well the stranger, as he that is born in
the land."‡ Caiaphas declares that the law has spoken, and that he will
see that its sentence be speedily carried out.

A shout of approval from the Council closes this long and remarkable scene, in which the law is appealed to against Him who gave it, and
the High Priest, sitting in Moses' seat, condemns the Author and Source
of his authority.

It is followed by the scene in the hall of the High Priest, which is
full of maid-servants and men. St. John comes to the door and asks
leave to bring in Peter. The acting of Hett (St. Peter) in this scene is
most striking and instructive, and he *looks* his part better than any actor.
He stands facing the audience, over the fire which has been made in the
middle of the hall, warming his hands, with an expression in which
anxiety, grief, and fear are mingled. The latter predominates as he hears
the servants discussing the attack on Malchus by one of the followers of
Jesus, and agreeing that it will be a case of "ear for ear ;" so that his
answer to the first maid-servant seems almost the natural result of his
condition. "I have been watching thee for a long time," she says. "If
I do not mistake, thou art one of the disciples of the Galilæan?" "I?

* Deut. xvii. 12.   † Ex. xxxi. 14.   ‡ Lev. xxiv. 15, 16.

No—I am not! Woman, I know Him not, nor do I know even what thou sayest." He instantly tries to slip out of the hall, but comes against the maid who keeps the door. The difference between the frightened, hesitating manner of his first denial and his strong protestation later is strikingly brought out, especially when, the third time, he lifts his eyes and hands to heaven, and with vehement action swears by the living God, "I know not the Man of whom ye speak." At this moment the Christus is led into the hall, and for a moment the Master and disciple are face to face ; then Peter leaves the hall, and the curtain falls.

The scene which followed, of Peter bewailing his sin, was to me one of the most instructive and touching in the play ; loving repentance could hardly be more deeply expressed both in word and action, nor the *instant* return of the soul to Him whom it had left ; horror of self only increasing trust in His forgiveness and mercy. I give the whole of the words, as I wrote them down afterwards in Hett's cottage ; they may recall to others the action and passion of mourning love with which they were spoken.

"O dearest Master! how deeply have I fallen! O weak, O wretched man ! Thee, my most loving Friend and Teacher, I have denied—three times have I denied Thee for whom I promised to die ! Oh, I know not how I could so terribly have forgotten myself! Accursed be my shameful betrayal ! May my heart be ever filled with sorrow for this despicable cowardice ! Lord, my dearest Lord ! if Thou hast still grace left for me, grace for a faithless one, oh grant it, grant it even to me ! Even now hearken to the voice of my repentant heart. Alas! the sin has been committed ; I can never more undo it, but ever, ever will I weep and repent over it ; never, never more will I leave Thee ! O Thou most full of goodness, Thou wilt not cast me out ? Thou wilt not despise my bitter repentance ? No ; the gentle, compassionate glance with which Thou didst look on me, thy deeply fallen disciple, assures me that Thou wilt forgive me. This hope I have in Thee, O best of Teachers. And the whole love of my heart shall from this moment belong to Thee, and keep me most closely united to Thee. Nothing, nothing shall be able ever again to separate me from Thee ! "

O felix culpa ! we are almost inclined to exclaim, which could lead to such love and repentance ; but yet we rather feel : O blessed glance, which in a moment could burn up self and fears for self, and trust in self, and kindle a life-long flame of devotion, fed by the remembrance of that hour, until love should triumph over torture and death, uniting him at last and forever on the cross to Him whom for a moment he had forsaken.

In the next scene the Christus is mocked by twenty-four soldiers of the High Priest during the night so spent by Him in preparation for the sufferings of the next day. He is blindfolded, smitten, pushed from his seat, so that he falls on the ground ; but throughout he preserves dignity, meek endurance, and perfect silence.

The tenth act opens with the tableau of Cain, in an attitude of despair, his hand pressed to his brow, standing over the slain body of Abel. Cain is clad in a leopard's skin, Abel in a sheepskin. Immediately after this tableau Judas appears, despair gnawing at his heart. "No hope! no escape!" he cries out in horror. "If the Master had willed to save Himself, He would have made them feel His power a second time in the garden." He rails at the accursed Synagogue, at the traders, at himself, and rushes away declaring that he will have no part in the blood of the innocent. His remorse, face to face with his sin, is a fearful contrast to the repentance of Peter.

The Sanhedrim is assembled, and as Caiaphas is telling the Council that he could not wait for morning to complete the condemnation of the enemy of the law, Judas bursts in, and the last terrible scene between him and his tempters takes place. It is but the drawing out of the Scripture account : "What is that to us ? see thou to that." His despair is only treated with indifference, and his rage sternly rebuked. "Have ye condemned Him ?" he asks in agony. "He must die," is thundered in his ears by the whole assembly. "Woe! woe!" he shrieks forth ; "I have sinned, I have betrayed the righteous. O ye bloodthirsty judges, ye condemn and destroy the innocent!" "Peace, Judas, or——" "No peace for me for evermore," he breaks out ; "no peace for you! The blood of the innocent cries for vengeance." In vain he is admonished as to the respect due to the High Priest and the Council ; despair raises him above them ; and when reminded that he made his own bargain, has duly received his reward, and that if he behaves himself he may have something further, he cries out with intense horror : "I will have nothing more! I tear asunder the shameful compact : let the innocent go free. I demand His freedom—my hands shall be pure from His blood." Then, when sternly told, "Thy Master must die, and thou hast delivered Him to death," he shrieks out, "Die!—I am a traitor! May ten thousand devils from hell tear me in pieces. Here, ye blood-hounds, take your accursed blood-money," and with terrible action and increasing rage and despair he flings the bag of silver at the feet of Caiaphas ; "body and soul are lost, and ye—ye shall be dragged with me into the lowest abyss of hell."

There is a pause after he has rushed from the Council ; even Caiaphas seems for a moment appalled, and exclaims, "A fearful man!" but quickly collecting himself, says, "He has betrayed his Friend ; we pursue our Enemy."

Again the Christus is led in ; and the Gospel story in St. Luke xxiii. 66-71, is exactly represented. Annas asks him, "Art thou the Christ ? tell us:" and the answer is given, "If I tell you, ye will not believe ; and if I also ask you, ye will not answer me, nor let me go." And when the last answer of truth is given, "Ye say that I am," the horrible cry again breaks forth: "He must die!" and three members of the Council are sent to Pilate to ask him to pass judgment before the feast.

The act closes with the final despair of Judas—a wonderful and fearful scene, the acting of which would alone, it has been said by considerable critics, give Lechner a high place among the actors of Europe. His monologue, written by Daisenberger, is in sharpest contrast to that of Peter. Both see the full horror of their sin: but one sees it in the light of his Master's countenance, healing while it wounded; the other in the hopeless blackness which he had voluntarily chosen. "I am cast away," he cries, "hated and abhorred by all, even by those who led me astray; I wander alone with this inward devouring fire. Oh, if I dared but once more to see His face; I might yet cling to Him, the only anchor of salvation! But He is in prison—is perhaps already put to death; no hope, no hope for me! He is dead, and I am His murderer! Cursed be the hour when my mother brought me forth! Here, accursed life, will I end thee! let the most miserable of all fruit hang on this tree." The curtain falls as he tears off his girdle.

The eleventh act, of Christ before Pilate (prefaced by the tableau of Daniel accused before Darius), calls forth all Johann Lang's powers. It is a grand scene: on the left of the balcony of Pilate's house the assembly of the scribes and priests; on the right the Christus amid his guards, and on the balcony the noble figure of Pilate in his magnificent dress surrounded by his court. Before he appears, Caiaphas again stirs up and exhorts the Council, reminds them that the whole peace of their country depends on this moment, charges them to be firm in their resolve, and not to rest till their enemy is put to death. It is wonderful how he overcomes the difficulty of addressing and haranguing Pilate from *below*, and how the stronger will seems to reverse their positions and make Caiaphas the dominating figure. He pays a brief and haughty homage to the viceroy of Cæsar when he appears, and instantly proceeds to demand judgment on the Prisoner.

The Scripture narrative is followed, but with additions. On Pilate's first declaration that he cannot condemn a man without knowing whether he is guilty, a Rabbi informs him that the whole Council have given judgment against him, and that it is therefore hardly worth his while to inquire into the case. "What!" he replies, "ye dare to propose to me, the representative of Cæsar, to become a blind tool for carrying out your resolutions. That be far from me! I must know what law he has broken, and in what manner."

The long struggle between Caiaphas and Pilate then begins, the latter clearly seeing through the malice of the accusers. When Caiaphas asks if the title of "King of Israel" is not rebellion against Cæsar, Pilate replies with derision: "I marvel at your suddenly aroused zeal for the honour of Cæsar." When he commands that the Prisoner be brought into his house, that he may question Him alone, a Rabbi says, "This is a dangerous delay." But Caiaphas answers, "Do not lose courage! Victory belongs to the steadfast!"

The first and second conversation with Pilate given in St. John's Gospel (before and after the Scourging) are in the "Passions-Spiel" given in one, beginning with the second. "Whence art Thou?" Pilate asks; and receiving no answer, continues, "Speakest thou not unto me? Knowest thou not that I have power to crucify Thee, and have power to release Thee?" Then at length the Christus speaks: "Thou couldest have no power at all against Me, except it were given thee from above; therefore he that delivered Me unto thee hath the greater sin."* "A bold speech," Pilate says aside; then, to the Christus, "Art thou the King of the Jews?" The rest of the conversation exactly follows St. John xviii. 34-38.

The words, "Thou sayest that I am a king," were spoken by Mayr with perhaps a too royal bearing, with a rather haughty raising of the head, and the very slightest approach to theatrical effect. It is easy to see throughout, that what is grand and royal would naturally best suit Mayr's acting; admirable as is his rendering of meekness and endurance, we feel that the man himself speaks out more truly in the parts where authority are expressed.

We marvel how Rendl (Pilate) has learnt to bear himself so nobly, or to say the famous words, "What is truth?" with that sudden, dreamy, inward expression and tone as though outward circumstances had for an instant vanished from his mind, and he were alone with his own soul and with the flood of thought raised by the words of Christ. To the message of his wife, which is now brought to him, he replies that she may be without anxiety, as he does not intend to give way to the Jews, and takes counsel with his courtiers, who declare their belief that envy alone is the cause of the accusations against Christ. When the crowd of priests return beneath his balcony, he says decidedly, "He is guiltless;" but yet continues to parley with them, condescends to excuse himself for not yielding, and at length catches eagerly at the mention of Galilee to send the prisoner to Herod.

An admirable tableau of Samson, destroying his enemies by his death, preceded the twelfth act. The unconcern of a group to the left was especially striking, continuing a game while the pillars were even then giving way. The scene of Christ before Herod was possibly a little too lengthened, yet if so, this is only through the faithfulness of the Ammergauers to the Gospel history. Herod questions with Him "in many words," while Caiaphas and the chief priests, following their victim, who is now guarded by Roman soldiers to this new tribunal, "vehemently accuse Him." They are terribly in earnest, but fail in persuading the pleasure-

---

* St. John xix. 9-11.

loving Herod to take the matter seriously ; he positively refuses to give any judgment except that the Christ is a simple man, not clever enough for the crimes laid against Him.

There are two tableaux before the thirteenth act—the bloody coat of Joseph shown to his father, while the Chorus sing :—

So wird auch Jesu Leib zerrissen ;*

and Isaac upon the Altar of Sacrifice. In the first scene the struggle between Pilate and Caiaphas begins again, as the latter stands beneath the balcony at the head of the Council ; the Christus on the other side. Pilate proposes to scourge Him, "in order," he says, "to meet your wishes," and release Him. But Caiaphas declares that the law requires that He should be put to death. Pilate then stakes all upon one venture, evidently with no doubt of its success. He has heard of the triumphant entry into Jerusalem, and it is clear that he regards the Christus as a popular idol, knowing that the priests "for envy had delivered Him."

To the people therefore he determines to appeal, pledging himself to abide by their decision. The part of Pilate could not have been written without fine appreciation of his character and motives, and it forms a most suggestive commentary on the text of the Gospels.

"Ye force me to tell you openly what I think," he says. "Moved by ignoble passion, ye persecute this Man, because the people are better disposed towards Him than towards you. I have listened long enough to your envious complaints, I will now hear the voice of the people." He then says that he shortly expects the people to assemble in order to demand, according to custom, the release of a prisoner, and promises to allow their choice between Jesus and Barabbas to be final. "It will then be shown," he says confidently, "whether your complaints are the expression of the mind of the people, or only of your own rage." Caiaphas, no less confident in his power over the fickle mob, bows, and replies haughtily, "It will then be seen, O Governor, that thou hast wrongly thought evil of us ;" while the whole Council cry out, "Release unto us Barabbas, and crucify this Man." But Pilate answers firmly, "Ye are not the people. The people will decide. Meanwhile I will cause Him to be scourged."

The action and words of Caiaphas, after Pilate has retired, are appalling in their bitter determination to pursue his Victim to the death. "Pilate has appealed to the people," he says ; "well, we will also appeal to them." He bids the priests to disperse themselves through the whole of Jerusalem, and to "move the people, that he should rather release Barabbas unto them." Every obstacle only feeds the flame of his fiery zeal ; what is indicated by a few words in St. Mark is represented in most impressive action. "Let us not lose a moment," he exclaims ; "let us go

* " Even thus is Jesu's body torn."

and meet the crowd, to excite and inflame them. Try to kindle in them the most glowing hatred against the enemy of Moses. Seek to win the wavering through the power of your words and promises. Terrify the followers of the Galilæan by scorn and reproach, by threats, and if necessary by ill-usage, so that not one may dare to come here, much less to open his mouth."

The traders take an active part in carrying out these commands ; we are never allowed to lose sight of the working of their revenge amongst the causes of the condemnation of Christ.

The scene of the scourging and crowning with thorns concludes this act.

A gorgeous tableau, of Joseph made ruler over Egypt, introduces the fourteenth act ; and a second tableau, of the two goats as sin-offerings, was also amongst the most striking.

The words of the Chorus become more and more touching, and full of instruction. We have just beheld the King of Israel, with the crown wherewith His mother (the Jewish nation) crowned Him ; while in mournful accents the Chorus sang :—

> How shall His Godhead now appear ?
> Alas ! behold the Man !
> A worm, the scorn of soldiers now.

But as the curtain rises and discloses the triumph of Joseph, the strain is changed to one of joy :—

> Behold the Man !
> See Joseph called to high estate ;
> Behold the Man !
> The type, in pain and joy, of Christ.

During the tableau of the goat slain as a sin-offering, they sing of the new Offering required for the pardon of sin :—

> A Lamb, from every blemish pure ;

and then suddenly break off their song, and for the first time actually take part in the drama ; the Choragus exclaiming, while fierce cries are heard in the distance :—

> The murderer's fearful cry I hear.

> Barabbas be our choice to-day,

is thundered forth by the unseen multitude.

> No, Jesus be from fetters free,

the Chorus sings in unison.

> Ah ! fiercer sounds the murderous cry,

is intoned by the Choragus.

"Crucify Him! crucify Him!" is heard louder and nearer, as the crowd press on, though still unseen.

In vain the Chorus plead :—

> Jerusalem ! Jerusalem !
> God will avenge the blood of His Son !

> His blood be on us, and on our children,

is the response.

> Be it then upon you and upon your children,

is solemnly intoned by the Choragus ; and the curtain rises. Again, as in the first scene, the crowd pour forth from the streets of Jerusalem, animated by one passionate sentiment. They are in four bands, led respectively by Annas, Caiaphas, and two of the chief priests, Nathanael and Ezechiel, and gather into one dense crowd beneath Pilate's balcony, acting and speaking as one man. "He has blasphemed God !" "To death with the false Prophet !" "Crucify Him !" "Release unto us Barabbas !" "The Nazarene must die !"—such is the burden of "their rude lawless cry ;" until Pilate appears on the balcony with the Christus, "wearing the purple robe and the crown of thorns ;" and there is a moment's pause as he pronounces the words, "Behold the Man !"

Pilate is still confident in the success of his appeal to the people ; and when the cry of "Crucify Him !" is still raised, orders Barabbas to be brought forth, and the Christus to be placed beside him. Then, as the two stand side by side beneath his balcony, and the crowd exclaim, "Let the Nazarene die !" he cannot contain his disappointment and astonishment. "I do not comprehend this people : a few days ago they followed this Man, rejoicing and applauding Him, through the streets of Jerusalem. Is it possible that the same people should now demand His death and destruction ?"

Caiaphas replies, that the eyes of the people have been opened, and a shout is raised, "Let Him die ! The false Messiah, the deceiver !"

One last effort is made by Pilate. Pointing to the two prisoners respectively, he bids the people consider and choose—choose between the noble, gentle Figure of Him whom they have long honoured as a wise Teacher, and who now, though without fault, bears the marks of cruel chastisement, and the frightful figure of the robber and murderer. "I appeal to your good sense, to your feeling as men. Choose! Whom will ye that I release unto you, Barabbas or Jesus which is called Christ ?"

Then the last fearful cry is raised : "Away with this Man, and deliver unto us Barabbas !" and Caiaphas eagerly reminds Pilate of his promise. "I am accustomed to keep my word without needing a reminder," he answers ; yet still struggles against the will which is overpowering his sense of justice. But his plea, "Shall I crucify your King ?" only leads to the arguments and threats to which he at last succumbs. He cannot face the fear of Cæsar's displeasure.

All this scene is really magnificently acted by both Caiaphas and Pilate. The most august trial in the world's history is represented before us ; and yet we are not disappointed, but held spell-bound by awe and overpowering interest. We know what the bitter end will be, and yet can scarce believe that it will come. Can this noble and clear-sighted Roman judge yield indeed to the clamour of the mob ? Will he endure the threat, " We will not leave the place until judgment is given ? " Can even the mob choose Barabbas ?

Yes, Barabbas is set free, and led away ; formal judgment is pronounced and written down by Pilate's secretary ; and then having washed his hands, declaring to the last the innocence of his Prisoner, he commands the two thieves to be brought forth. They stand beside the noble figure of the Christus, and the sentence is read. Then Pilate says, " Now take ye Him, and——" he pauses, as though unable to speak the words, but at length they seem forced from him, and breaking his staff of office in two, he exclaims, in a tone of anger and despair, " Crucify Him ! " He too has made the great choice, and turning hastily, almost rushes from the judgment-seat.

" To Golgotha ! " is shouted, and a tumultuous procession is formed— One alone moving calmly and peacefully, though in bonds, and amid every mark of deepest indignity.

The Passions-Spiel began with the " Einzug," and now we have come to the " Kreuzweg." It is introduced by three tableaux : Isaac bearing the wood to Mount Moriah ; the children of Israel bitten by fiery serpents ; and the Brazen Serpent. Both of these latter are admirable in conception, in grouping and in colouring. There are a multitude of figures, numbers of them being children, and yet less than a minute elapses from the moment that the curtain falls on the first until it rises on the second. Moses is, of course, the central figure in the last tableau ; he is represented by Flunger, who was the Christus of 1850.

The first lines sung by the Chorus before these tableaux are amongst the most solemn and impressive both in words and music, although the latter is very simple :—

> Pray and render heartfelt thanks !
> He who drank the bitter cup
> Follows now the paths of death,
> Reconciling man to God.

Even more moving and overcoming than the Crucifixion is the Way of the Cross. The procession advances slowly from the right, met by the group from Bethany from the left, and by Simon of Cyrene and the Women of Jerusalem, in the middle stage. Far more impressive and noble than in the hour of triumph is the Figure bending beneath the Cross, each step evidently a struggle with mortal weakness, and yet moving "calm as the march of some majestic cloud" amidst the brutality and jeers of the crowd. He falls beneath the Cross, but it is with unruffled anguish; He tries even in falling to support the burden laid upon Him: we feel that the worn body is doing its utmost to obey the cruel behests of His tormentors.

It is, I think, the scene which of all in the play speaks most touchingly to a Christian's heart, making us feel as we never did before: "What should all pain be to us but a joyful treading in those Footprints?"

The Christus has spoken no word since He said to Pilate, "Every one that is of the truth heareth My words;" but now, as Simon of Cyrene is willingly laden with the Cross, He opens His mouth in benediction. "The blessing of God be on thee and thine," He says in a voice faint with exhaustion and anguish, and moves slowly on to meet the Women of Jerusalem, Veronica and the Maries, with St. John. The latter follow on the way of the Cross, as the august procession passes out of sight.

There is a pause after the curtain has fallen, and the painful strain is almost more than we can bear, as the Chorus, clad now in black, file slowly in, and while the sound of blows with a hammer are heard behind the scenes, mournfully chant:—

> Come, pious souls, draw near the Lamb,
> Who freely gives Himself for you.
> Behold Him on the Tree of doom,
> Between two murderers He hangs;
> He, Son of God, His life-blood gives,—
> And ye no tears give back to Him?

When the curtain rises the two thieves are already tied to their crosses, which are upright; but in the centre a prostrate Form lies nailed to a cross, which has not yet been raised. There is a delay, while a messenger from Pilate brings in the handwriting which is to proclaim the Sufferer a King even upon this cruel throne; then the cross is slowly raised.

I was almost too near the first time that we saw this awful representation. It may be also that the very excellence of representations of the Crucifix, to which we are accustomed both in sculpture and painting, makes this living picture less striking than are other parts of the Passion Play. I think that this is in great measure owing to the flesh-coloured garment which entirely covers the body, and beneath which it is evidently tightly laced in some sort of stays. For there is no expansion of the chest or of the muscles such as would naturally be caused by the position, and which we see represented in even the rudest crucifix. The chest is quite flat, and gives the impression, when seen very near, of being tightly bound to the cross, as it doubtless is, by the stays which confine the body. The feet are covered by the "tricot," the edges of which are clearly seen at the neck and wrists, which are uncovered ; and there is a great contrast between its colour and that of the skin, especially as the hands soon become almost purple from the binding of the wrists. All this, especially the clothed feet, certainly rather diminished the effect on the mind as we gazed on the motionless Form so awfully familiar to us in sculpture.

But all was changed when the head, which hung slightly to the right, was slowly lifted, the eyes raised to heaven, and the first words uttered. This single movement and expression of countenance seemed to me the greatest and noblest in Mayr's acting. The picture at that moment is still before my eyes ; it can never pass away. All was forgotten except the Head and Countenance, and the words spoken ; and all this was perfect. The whole of the scene recorded in Scripture was acted around the Cross : the mockery ; the soldiers parting the raiment ; the attempt of Caiaphas to induce Pilate to remove the superscription ; the conversion of the Centurion. But now we could see nothing but the thorn-crowned Head, and watch for the words which fell at intervals from the Sufferer's lips. Nothing could be more perfect than the weary, agonized, but tender movement of the head, as he turned it from Mary to St. John. Each utterance marked a stage of suffering and desolation, and the time seemed rather hours than minutes, until the eyes, full of anguish and of love, were for the last time raised to Heaven, and the last words spoken.

> Love masters agony : the soul that seemed
> Forsaken, feels her present God again :
> And in her Father's arms
> Contented dies away.

" And all the people that came together to that sight, beholding the things which were done, smote their breasts, and returned." This instantaneous change of feeling in the crowd, which had been worked up by the chief priests, was acted so as to make us realize it as we had never done before. Only Caiaphas remains firm and unchanged. Even the tidings brought hastily to him of the rent veil of the Temple fail to move him, though the other priests are evidently disturbed by some misgivings. His resentment against Him whom he has destroyed only becomes keener, and he exclaims, pointing fiercely to the Cross, " He has brought this to pass by his wicked enchantments."

Beneath the close-fitting garment worn by the Christus there was visible, from a very short distance, the mark of what looked like a small, shield-like plate over the heart. I had imagined that some kind of bladder was worn in this spot, which could be pierced by the spear, and was puzzled by this plate, which attracted the eye, as the sharp hard edges were clearly marked. But I learned afterwards that the spearhead contains the blood-coloured fluid which seems to flow from the pierced side, and is so contrived that when it is pressed against a hard surface it gives way, and an aperture is made, through which the fluid gushes out, apparently from the heart, against which the spear is pressed.

At some distance the effect of the pierced hands was perfectly given, but from very near the stage it was easy to perceive that the nails passed between the fingers, and were then bent so that the very large nail-heads covered the centre of the palm, while the third and little fingers were closed so as to conceal the crooked part of the nail. I believe also that a broad band passes over each wrist, under the "tricot," and is then fastened to the cross; there were many marks of nails clearly visible (after the taking down from the cross) at the spot where the wrists would come, besides the larger marks, nearer the end, of the nails of the hands.

Caiaphas and the chief priests, who had left the scene on the news of the rending of the veil, return with persistent hatred to avenge, as Caiaphas says, "the destruction wrought in the Temple," on the lifeless body of the Christ. But the limit of his power has been reached, and the victory of death begins. In vain he curses Nicodemus and Joseph of Arimathea, forbidding them ever again to appear in the Council. They are strong in the authority of the Roman Governor, and, renouncing their allegiance to the Sanhedrim, boldly guard the sacred body.

For scenic effect the taking down from the Cross is perhaps the most beautiful in the Passions-Spiel both in grouping and action, and is quite marvellous in the tenderness of every movement and every incident. The chief actors are both on ladders, and in positions which might easily become grotesque. They have also to accomplish not only what is seen, the extracting of the nails and lifting down of the body, but the unfastening of the unseen bandages. Yet all is so done by these true artists as to make the whole scene one of exquisite beauty. Nothing can be more tenderly reverent than the laying down of the body on Mary's knees, or the slow, mournful procession to the grave.

Here, it has been felt by some, the Passions-Spiel might end; but though it is true that the few scenes which follow are poor in comparison of what has gone before, yet I think that they are necessary both to complete the argument of the play and to lighten the feeling of profound sadness which has so long oppressed the audience. Without the Resurrection the drama would be incomplete. When the chorus of Schutzgeister once more appears in many-coloured robes, we feel that joy and hope are at hand. They sing :—

> Liebe, Liebe, in dem Blute
> Kampftest du mit Gottes Muthe.*

And continue :—

> Softly rest, O Sacred Frame,
> In the stillness of the grave ;
> All thy bitter passion o'er !
> In earth's lap, O softly rest
> Till Thy glory be revealed.

---

* "Love, O Love, in Thy dear blood,
  Thou didst strive with God's own might."

> Never shall corruption's worm
> Touch or mar Thy holy flesh.

The scenes of the guarded grave, the Resurrection, the women at the sepulchre, and even of the meeting of the Magdalene with her risen Master, are all of the second order, and not to be compared with those before the Resurrection; but when, after the Christus has left Mary, she exclaims, "Hallelujah! He is risen," and the cry is echoed on all sides, as the Schutzgeister enter for the last time, the hearts of the audience respond to the song of joy and triumph chanted during the closing tableau which has taken the place of the scene of the Ascension. This last is not now attempted, but the Christus is seen for the last time standing on a mount in white and glistening raiment, holding in his hand the Resurrection banner. His enemies are made his footstool, and cower beneath his feet, while around him are grouped his friends, and many of the typical figures from the Old Testament tableaux. Even as we looked a ray of brilliant sunshine suddenly broke out and illumined the countenance and figure of the Christus. So we saw him for the last time, while the Hallelujahs of the Chorus pealed forth :—

> The Hero hath conquered,
> The might of the foe!
> Few hours in the grave,
> In the gloom hath He slept.
> Sing before Him holy Psalms!
> Strew before Him Conquerors' palms.
> The Lord He hath risen!
> Break forth, O ye heavens,
> Earth, sing to the Victor,
> To Him who hath risen!
> Hallelujah!

Even more beautiful and touching than the greeting of the Chorus was their farewell: "Let us behold, ere we part, the triumphant festival of victory. Now, in majesty and great glory, He enters the New Jerusalem, where He will gather to Himself all whom He hath purchased with His blood. Strengthened and full of joy at this sight, return to your homes, O friends, filled with tenderest love for Him Who loved you even unto death, and still loves you eternally in heaven; there, where the song of victory ever resounds, Praise be to the Lamb Who was slain! There, reunited around our Saviour, we shall all meet again. Hallelujah!"

"On His head are many crowns." Yet may we not reverently believe that He Who on earth chose the homage of the poor, accepts the crown laid at His feet by these simple and pious souls? Not of them can it be said that they have done the work of the Lord negligently. For many generations they have not only steadily and patiently performed their vow, but have brought to the performance that earnest purpose of doing their best, through which all true art has been matured. The

Passion Play and its traditions have been the very life of the village ; each child born there hears of it and prepares for his part in it from infancy ; while to personate the Christus or the Mutter-Gottes is the highest distinction to which any youth or maiden dreams of attaining.

Most gladly would we have lingered in this delightful valley, and have increased our acquaintance with its inhabitants. Alas! the time for farewells had come, and we had but an hour on Tuesday morning to visit those who had become as friends, and to bid them adieu.

Last and chiefest among these was the Geistlicher Rath. When we called he had just returned from church, and was sitting with Arvisenet's "Memoriale Vitæ Sacerdotis" open before him. He received us with even more kindly warmth than before, and seemed pleased with our delight with his village and people. He said, "You must return in ten years, but you will not find me here : " then he talked of the actors, saying that just now he knew of no one who could take Mayr's part, but that of course there were always some growing up in the village who might be fit to undertake it ten years hence, and that in any case he did not see why Mayr should not take it again, as he is now only thirty-three. He told us that Flunger's representation of the Christus had been a wholly different one from Mayr's, but, "very good, very good." To our expressions of regret at leaving Ober-Ammergau he answered quickly and brightly, "Then stay. Bleiben Sie doch ! "

Certainly not the least part of our regret was the feeling that we were bidding a last farewell to the venerable old man who had inspired us with deep respect and admiration—who, with no object but the glory of God and the improvement of his people, had given his best years to patient and profound study of the Passion of his Master, and of the best means of drawing out its lessons for the benefit of his flock, and enabling them to do that which they had vowed in the best and highest way.

It is not too much to say that the result of his work has become the wonder and delight of Christendom. Let us hope that to many and many a soul it has been much more—that the scenes they have witnessed have not been to them only a marvellous art-performance, or the choruses heard only as the very lovely song of one that hath a pleasant voice ; but that thousands of hearts have responded to the earnest efforts of the performers to make their Play a religious exercise, and to provide matter for deep meditation and instruction.

If the lessons so taught be even a little recalled or deepened by this slight record of impressions received in the theatre of Ober-Ammergau, it will not have been written in vain.

THE WORDS

OF

THE PASSION PLAY

TRANSLATED INTO ENGLISH.

The Drama is divided into Three Parts, containing in all Seventeen Acts. Each Act is preceded by one or more Tableaux from the Old Testament, and by a Prologue, spoken by the Choragus.

The first Two Parts each consist of Seven Acts; the Third Part of Three Acts and a final Tableau.

THE PASSION PLAY.

PART I.

From Christ's Entry into Jerusalem to His being taken Captive in the Garden of Gethsemane.

ACT I.

PROLOGUE.

Enter the Chorus or Schutzgeister (*see* pp. 5, 6). The Choragus (or leader of the Chorus) exhorts the spectators to a devout contemplation of the holy Drama, explaining its great lesson—God reconciled to man through Christ. "All hail!" he says, welcome to the band of brothers, whom love divine hath here assembled, who wish to share the sorrows of their Saviour, and to follow Him, step by step, on the way of His sufferings to the Cross and the Sepulchre. He intones and sings :—

Wirf zum heiligen Staunen dich nieder, Von Gottes Fluch gebeugtes Geschlecht! Friede dir! aus Sion Gnade wieder!	In holy wonder cast thee down, O race oppressed by God's own curse! Peace be to thee! From Sion peace once more!
Nicht ewig zürnt Er, Der Beleidigte—ist sein Zürnen gleich gerecht.	He is not wroth for aye, The offended One—His wrath is ever just.
" Ich will"—so spricht der Herr— " Den Tod des Sünders nicht—vergeben " Will Ich ihm—er soll leben! " Versöhnen wird ihn selbst Meines Sohnes Blut, versöhnen !" Preis, Anbetung, Freudenthränen, Ewiger Dir!	" I desire not," thus saith The Lord, " the sinner's death—I will Forgive him—he shall live again ! My Son's own blood shall reconcile him." Praise, worship, tears of joy to Thee, Eternal !
Doch, Heiligster, darf der Staub sich unterstehn, Hin in der Zukunft Heiligthum zu sehn?	Yet, Holiest, shall the dust now dare Into the Future's Sanctuary to gaze?

D

The Curtain rises and discloses the

FIRST TABLEAU.—THE EXPULSION FROM PARADISE. (*See* p. 7.)

The Chorus sings.

Die Menschheit ist verbaunt aus Eden's Au'n	From Eden's groves mankind is driven,
Von Sünd' umnachtet und von Todes-Grau'n.	Sin's night, and death's dread terror bound him,
Ihr ist zum Lebensbaum—der Eingang ach ! versperrt.	To the Tree of Life his way is barr'd,
Es drohet in des Cherub's Hand das Flammenschwert.	With flaming sword threatens the Cherub's hand.
Doch von ferne, von Calvaria's Höhen Leuchtet durch die Nacht ein Morgenglüh'n ;	Yet from afar, from Calvary's height, A morning gleam shines through the night,
Aus des Kreuzbaumes Zweigen wehen Friedenslüfte durch die Welten hin.	From the branches of the Tree of shame Through all worlds flow airs of balmy peace.
Gott ! Erbarmer ! Sünder zu begnaden, Die verachtet schändlich Dein Gebot, Gibst Du, von dem Fluche zu entladen, Deinen Eingebornen in den Tod.	God of Mercy ! sinners to forgive Who Thy law have shamefully despised, Thou dost give, to free them from the curse, Unto bitter death Thine only Son.

SECOND TABLEAU.—THE ADORATION OF THE CROSS. (*See* p. 7.)

Chorus (kneeling).

Ew'ger ! höre Deiner Kinder Stammeln ! Weil ein Kind ja nichts als stammeln kann ! Die beim grossen Opfer sich versammeln, Beten Dich voll heil'ger Erfurcht an.	Eternal ! hear Thy children's falt'ring prayer ! Only with stamm'ring lips a child can pray. They who gather round the mighty offering In holy veneration worship Thee.
Folget dem Versöhner nun zur Seite, Bis Er Seinen rauhen Dornenpfad Durchgelaufen, und im heissen Streite Blutend für uns ausgekämpfet hat.	Follow the Atoner now beside, Until He His rough and thorny path Hath fully run,—and in fiercest strife Bleeding fought for us, and won the fight.

CHRIST'S ENTRY INTO JERUSALEM.

SCENE I. (*See* pp. 7–9.)

A Multitude of People enter singing. JESUS *enters Jerusalem amid the rejoicing of the People, followed by the Disciples, who each carry a Pilgrim's Staff. The Children and People sing :—*

Heil Dir ! Heil Dir ! o Davids Sohn ! Heil Dir ! Heil Dir ! der Väter Thron Gebühret Dir.	Hail to Thee ! Hail ! O David's Son ! Hail to Thee ! Hail ! The Father's throne Belongs to Thee.
Der in des Höchsten Namen kömmt, Dem Israel entgegenströmt, Dich preisen wir.	Who cometh in the Highest's Name, Whom Israel onward throngs to meet, Thee we adore !

Hosanna ! der im Himmel wohnet,	Hosanna ! He Who dwells in Heav'n
Der sende alle Huld auf Dich.	All gracious favour pour on Thee.
Hosanna ! der dort oben thronet,	Hosanna ! He Who reigns above
Erhalte uns Dich ewiglich.	Preserve Thee ours for evermore.
Heil Dir, &c.	Hail to Thee, &c.
Gesegnet sei, Das neu auflebet,	Blessed be He, Who now restores
Des Vaters David Volk und Reich !	Our father David's seed and reign !
Ihr Völker segnet, preiset, hebet	Ye people, bless, praise, and exalt
Den Sohn empor, dem Vater gleich.	The Son, His Father's image true.
Heil Dir, &c.	Hail to Thee, &c.
Hosanna unserm Königssohne !	Hosanna to our royal Son !
Ertöne durch die Lüfte weit !	Resound on every breeze afar !
Hosanna ! auf des Vaters Throne	Hosanna ! On the Father's throne
Regiere Er voll Herrlichkeit !	Let Him in majesty aye rule.
Heil Dir, &c.	Hail to Thee, &c.

SCENE II.

CHRIST, *the* APOSTLES *and the* PEOPLE, PRIESTS, PHARISEES, *and* MERCHANTMEN, *in the Court of the Temple.*

Christ. What do I behold ?   Shall My Father's House be thus dishonoured ?   Is this the House of God ?   Or is it a market-place ?   Shall strangers, who come from heathen lands to worship God, perform their devotions here amidst this tumult of usury ?   And ye, O Priests, guardians of the sanctuary ! ye behold the iniquity, and suffer it ?   Woe unto you ! He, who searcheth the heart, knows wherefore ye permit this wrong.

Traders. Who then is this ?

People. It is the great Prophet of Nazareth in Galilee.

Christ (to the Traders). Go hence, ye servants of Mammon !   I command it.   Take that which is yours and depart from the Holy Place.

Priests. Why troublest Thou this people ?   All this is for sacrifice. How canst Thou forbid what the High Priest's Council permits ?

Traders. Are men no longer to offer sacrifices ?

Christ. Without the Temple are places sufficient for your business. My House, thus saith the Lord, shall be called a House of Prayer for all people !   But ye have made it a den of thieves. (*He overthrows the tables.*)   Take all this hence !

Traders. My money, alas, my money !   My doves ! (*The doves fly away.*)   Who will make good the loss to me ?

Christ (with a scourge of cords). Go hence ! I will that this consecrated place be given back to the worship of the Father !

Priests. What signs showest Thou that Thou hast power to do these things ?

Christ. Ye seek after signs! Yea, a sign shall be given unto you: destroy this temple and in three days I will raise it up.

Priests. What boastful words! Forty and six years was this temple in building and wilt Thou raise it up in three days?

People. Blessed be He that cometh in the name of the Lord!

Priests. Hearest Thou what these say? Rebuke Thy disciples.

Christ. I say unto you, If these should hold their peace, the stones would cry out.

Children. Hosanna to the Son of David!

Pharisees. Will ye be silent, ye simple ones?

Christ. Have ye never read, Out of the mouth of babes and sucklings Thou hast perfected praise? The things which are hidden from the proud are revealed unto babes. And the Scripture must be fulfilled: the stone which the builders refused is become the headstone of the corner: the Kingdom of God shall be taken from you, and shall be given unto a people that shall bring forth the fruits thereof. But that stone—whosoever shall fall upon it shall be broken, but on whomsoever it shall fall, it shall grind him to powder. Come, my disciples! I have done as the Father gave me commandment, I have vindicated the honour of His House. The darkness remains darkness; but in many hearts the day star will soon arise. Let us go into the sanctuary, that we may there pray unto the Father.   [*Exit.*

People. Praise to the Anointed!

Priests. Be silent, ye worthless ones!

Pharisees. Ye shall all fall with Him.

People. Blessed be the Kingdom of David, which again appears!

SCENE III.

PRIESTS *and* PEOPLE.

Nathanael. Let him who still holds with our Fathers Abraham, Isaac, and Jacob, be on our side! Let the curse of Moses be on all others!

Rabbi. He is a Deceiver!

People. Why have ye not taken Him? Is He not a Prophet? (*Some of the people go out after* JESUS.)

Priests. He is a teacher of evil!

Nathanael. O thou blind people! wilt thou go after one who is new, and wilt thou forsake Moses, the Prophets, and thy Priests? Fearest thou not the curse which falls upon deserters? Will ye cease to be the chosen people?

People. We will not!

Nathanael. Who has to watch over purity of teaching? Is it not the holy Sanhedrim of the people of Israel? Whom will ye hear, us, or Him, who gives Himself out as the proclaimer of a new teaching?

People. We will hear you—we will follow you!

Priests. The God of your Fathers will bless you for it.

SCENE IV.

Enter the TRADERS, *the* "CHIEF TRADER," DATHAN, *at their head, making a tumult.*

Traders. This fellow must be punished. Vengeance! He shall pay for His audacity. Money, oil, salt, doves,—He must make good everything! Wherever He is He shall feel our revenge!

Priests. He has departed.

Traders. We will go after Him.

Nathanael. Stay, friends! The following of this Man is still too great; a dangerous fight might take place, to which the sword of the Romans would make an end. Trust us: He shall not escape His punishment.

Priests. With us, and for us, that is your welfare.

All. Our victory is near!

Nathanael. We are now going hence to inform the Council of the High Priests of to-day's events.

Traders. We will go with you. We must have satisfaction.

Nathanael. In an hour come to the Court of the *High Priests.* I will bring your complaint before the Council and plead for you.

[*Exeunt the Priests.*

Traders and People (as they are departing). Moses is our Prophet! Praised be our fathers!

·ACT II.

COUNCIL OF THE HIGH PRIESTS. (*See* pp. 9, 10.)

PROLOGUE.

The Chorus enter from either side of the proscenium. The Choragus, after dwelling on the envy which moves the Pharisees to conspire against our Lord, and exhorting the spectators to give their hearts in thankfulness and attention to the drama, recites, in allusion to the last scene :—

Ha ! sind sie fort die losen Bösewichte—
Entlarvt die scheussliche Gestalt im vollen Lichte—
Die Tugendlappe von dem Sünderrock gerissen—
Gegeisselt von dem nagenden Gewissen.
"Auf ! lasset uns "—so schrei'n sie wild—
  "auf Rache sinnen,
Den längst entworfenen Plan beginnen !"

The wicked wretches now are gone—
In the full light the hideous shape unmasked—
The rags of virtue from sin's garment torn—
By gnawing conscience torn and scourged.
"Up, let us think on vengeance !" wild they cry ;
"Let us the long determined plot begin."

FIRST TABLEAU.—JOSEPH CAST INTO THE PIT BY HIS BRETHREN.

Chorus.

Eröffne, Gottheit, uns das Heiligthum !
Der Heuchler Plan malt uns das graue Alterthum,
Wie Jakobs Söhne gegen Joseph sich verschwören,
So werdet ihr von dieser Natterbrut
Bald über Jesus " Tod und Blut "
Voll Tigerrache rufen hören.

Sehet dort, der Träumer kömmt
Er will, schrei'n sie unverschämt,
Als ein König uns regieren.
Fort mit diesem Schwärmer, fort !

Ha ! in der Cisterne dort
Mag er seinen Plan ausführen.
So nach des Gerechten Blut
Dürstet jene Natterbrut.

Open, O Lord, to us Thy sanctuary !
Old times present to us deceiver's plans ;

As Jacob's sons 'gainst Joseph do conspire,

So shall ye of this viper brood
Full soon for Jesu's death and blood
The tigerish, vengeful outcry hear.

" See there, the dreamer comes ;
He wills," unshamed they cry,
" To rule us as a King.
Away with this fanatic !

" Ha ! there in that deep pit
May he his plan unfold :"
Thus for the just one's blood
Thirsteth that viper brood.

Er ist, schrei'n sie, uns entgegen :
Uns're Ehre liegt daran—
Alles ist ihm zugethan—
Wandelt nicht nach unsern Wegen.

Gott vertilge diese Frevler-Rotte,
Die sich wider Dich empört ;
Und den Mörderbund zum Spotte
Deines Eingebornen schwört.

Lasse Deiner Allmacht Donner brüllen,
Deine Rechte Blitze glüh'n,
Dass sie Deiner Rache Stärke fühlen,
Schmett're in den Staub sie hin.

"He is," they cry, "against us,
Our honour is at stake ;
All are gone after Him,
They follow us no more."

O God, destroy this evil band,
Who against Thee now rise up ;
And to murd'rous league, in scorn
Of Thine only Son, swear faith.

Let Almighty thunders peal,
Let Thy righteous lightning burn,
That they feel Thine anger's strength :
Strike them downward into dust !

A single Schutzgeister sings :—

Aber, nein, er kam nicht zum Verderben
Von des Vaters Herrlichkeit ;
Alle Sünder sollen durch Ihn erben
Gnade, Huld und Seligkeit.

No ! never came He to destroy,
From the Father's Majesty,
Sinners shall through Him inherit
Pardon, grace, and endless bliss.

Chorus.

Voll der Demuth beten dann
Deiner Liebe grossen Plan,
Gott ! wir Deine Kinder, an.

Humbly then we here adore
The great plan of Thy dear love,
We Thy children, O our God !

SCENE I.

The Members of the Sanhedrim.

Caiaphas. Venerable Brothers, Fathers, and Teachers of the People! An extra-ordinary occurrence is the extra-ordinary occasion of to-day's consultation. Hear it out of the mouth of our worthy brother.

Nathanael. Marvel not, O Fathers, that at so late an hour ye are called together for action. It is only too well known to you, what we have, to our shame, been forced to-day to behold with our own eyes. Ye have seen the triumphal procession of the Galilæan through the Holy City. Ye have heard the Hosanna of the befooled people ; ye have heard how this proud One has arrogated to Himself High Priestly dignity. What yet is wanting for the destruction of all civil and ecclesiastical order? Yet a few steps further, and the holy law of Moses is destroyed through the novelties of this teacher of error. The institutions of our Fathers are despised, fasts and purifyings done away with, the Sabbath desecrated, the Priests of God despoiled of their office, the holy sacrifices at an end.

All. Yea, verily, it is true.

Caiaphas. And yet more. Encouraged by His followers, He will give Himself out as King of Israel ; then will there be division in the land and rebellion against the Romans, and these will not delay to destroy both land and people. Woe to the children of Irsael, to the Holy City, to the Temple of the Lord! It is full time that the evil be exterminated. The responsibility lies upon us; even to-day a resolution must be taken, and what is resolved upon must be carried out without hesitation or looking back. Will ye put your hands to this work?

All. We will.

First Priest. A stop must be put to the doings of the Seducer.

Second Priest. We ourselves are partakers in the guilt in that it has gone so far. Against this overwhelming destruction too mild measures were used. What have our disputings with Him availed? What fruit has there been from our putting Him in a dilemma by questions? What has even been done by the excommunication pronounced upon any one who should acknowledge Him as Messias? If there is to be peace we must make sure of His person and put Him in prison.

All. Yea, that must be done.

Third Priest. If He is once in prison the credulous people will be no longer fascinated by the attraction of His presence and the magic of His words; and if they have no longer any wonder to gape at, all will soon be forgotten.

Fourth Priest. In the darkness of the dungeon He can let His light shine, and announce Himself as Messias to the prison walls.

First Pharisee. Long enough has He led the people astray, and branded as hypocrisy the strict virtue of the holy order of the Pharisees. Let Him expiate His misdeeds in bonds!

Second Pharisee. It will cool the fanaticism of His followers, if He, Who promised them freedom, Himself lie bound.

Annas. Now, venerable priests, a ray of comfort and joy once more warms my heart, since I see your unanimous resolution. Alas! an unspeakable sorrow weighed upon my soul at the sight of the onward course of the wrong teaching of this Galilæan. Have I, a miserable old man, only lived so long, in order to behold the overthrow of the sacred law? But now I will not lose courage. The God of our fathers still lives and is with us. If ye, fathers of the people, quit you like men, salvation is nigh. Have courage to be the saviours of Israel.

All. We are of one mind.

Priests. Israel must be saved.

Caiaphas. Honour to your unanimous resolution, worthy brethren. But now assist me with your wise counsels as to the surest way of getting this Deceiver into our power.

First Pharisee. To take Him now, on the feast day, would be too dangerous. In the streets and in the Temple, everywhere He is surrounded by a troop of insensate followers.

Priests. And yet it must be done at once; the matter allows of no delay. Perchance during the time of the feast He might raise an insurrection, and then it might happen that we should take the place which we have arranged for Him.

Other Priests. No delay!

Second Pharisee. We cannot now set to work altogether with open force, we must overcome Him quietly with guile. We must find out where He commonly spends the night, and so He could be surprised and brought into safe keeping without witnesses.

Nathanael. People will soon be found to track the fox to his hole, if it pleased the Council to offer a suitable reward.

Caiaphas. If ye, assembled fathers, think it good, I will, in the name of the Council, give the order that any one who knows His nightly resort should inform us of the same, and also a reward should be secured to the informant.

All. We agree entirely.

Nathanael. Doubtless those men could serve us as informers whom the Galilæan to-day, in the sight of all the people, has deeply injured. Before this they were jealous adherents of the law, and now they are thirsting for revenge against Him who has made such an unheard-of attack upon their privileges.

Caiaphas. Where are the traders to be found?

Nathanael. They are ready in the outer court. I have persuaded them to be the defenders of their rights before the holy Sanhedrim, and they await your orders.

Caiaphas. Worthy priest, announce to them that the Council is inclined to take up their grievance, and bring them in. [*Exit* NATHANAEL.

SCENE II.

Caiaphas. The God of our fathers has not yet withdrawn His hand from us. Moses yet watches over us. If we succeed in gathering around a knot of men out of the people I shall no longer fear. Friends and brothers! let us be of good courage, our fathers look down upon us from Abraham's bosom.

Priests. God bless our High Priest!

SCENE III.

Nathanael. High Priests and chosen Teachers! These men, worthy of our blessing, appear before this assembly, in order to bring a complaint against the well-known Jesus of Nazareth, who to-day in the Temple in an unheard-of manner has troubled them and caused them loss.

Traders. We beseech the Council to procure us satisfaction. The Council must protect our righteous demand.

Priests and Pharisees. Ye shall have satisfaction ; we will be your sureties for that.

Traders. Has not the Council given us leave to set out openly in the court all that is necessary for sacrifice ?

Priests. Yes, that we have permitted ; woe to him who disturbs you in this your right !

Traders. And the Galilæan has driven us out with a scourge ! And the tables of the money-changers has He overthrown, and emptied the dove-cages ! We demand satisfaction !

Caiaphas. That ye should have satisfaction the law decrees. Your loss shall meanwhile be made good to you out of the treasury of the Temple. But that the culprit himself should be punished, for this we need your co-operation. What can we do to Him so long as He is not in our power ?

Traders. He goes daily into the Temple ; there He can easily be taken prisoner and led away.

Caiaphas. That will not do. Ye know that He has a crowd of excited followers, and therefore a dangerous uproar might take place. It must be done quietly.

Traders. It would be best done in the night.

Caiaphas. If ye find out whither He withdraws Himself at night He will soon be in our hands without any tumult. Then ye will not only have the joy of seeing Him chastised but also a considerable recompense will be awarded to you.

Nathanael. Ye will also gain merit concerning the law of Moses.

Traders. On our part there shall be no failure. We will shun no trouble.

Chief Trader. I know one of His followers through whom I can easily accomplish something if I can offer him a corresponding reward.

Caiaphas. If thou findest out such a one make all promises to him in our name. Only delay not, in order that we may accomplish our end before the feast.

Annas. And observe strictest silence.

Traders. We swear it.

Caiaphas. If, however, good fellows, ye wish that the longing for vengeance should be fully satisfied, take also every possible trouble to kindle in many others the holy zeal which burns in you.

Traders. Since that occurrence, we have made use of every moment for this purpose, and many are already on our side. We will not rest till all the people rise up against Him !

Annas. By these means ye will lay the Council under an obligation of greatest gratitude.

Caiaphas. Ye will then be openly honoured by the whole people, as ye have been openly put to shame before them.

Traders. Our lives for the law of Moses and the holy Sanhedrim!
Caiaphas. The God of Abraham guide you!
Traders. Long live Moses! Long live the priests and the holy Sanhedrim! Even to-day may the Galilæan have played out His part. [*Exeunt.*

SCENE IV.

Caiaphas. As though strengthened by a sweet sleep I live once more! With such men all can be carried through. Now we shall see who will conquer: He, with His followers, to whom He unceasingly preaches love—a love which is to include even publicans and sinners; yea, and the heathen also—or we, with this troop, animated by hatred and revenge, which we send against Him.

Annas. May the God of our fathers grant us victory! How then will joy in my old age renew my youth!

Caiaphas. Let us break up. Praised be our fathers!

All. Praised be the God of Abraham, of Isaac, and of Jacob!

ACT III.

THE PARTING AT BETHANY.

PROLOGUE.

The Choragus explains the relation of the two tableaux to the leave-taking of Christ:—Who with clear gaze pierces the veil of the future, and already sees the gathering storm at hand, which threatens to discharge itself upon His head. While still amongst His own He speaks words to His beloved friends concerning separation—words, alas! which most bitterly wound His devoted Mother's soul. See with what deep trouble the mother of Tobias gazes after the departing son of her heart, and pours out her grief in streaming tears of tender love! Thus also the Mother of the Son of God laments her Beloved, who departs, determined to efface the sins of mankind through love's expiatory death! Behold the bride in the great Song of Solomon, how she complains: "The Bridegroom has disappeared!" How she calls and seeks and gives herself no rest till she find Him! Calmer is the anguish in Mary's soul; as a sword piercing her whole heart, yet softened through the pious resignation of trust in God. (*See* pp. 10, 11.)

Chorus.

Ach, sie kommt, die Scheidestunde,	Ah, they come, the parting hours !
Und sie schlägt die tiefste Wunde	Deepest wounds they now inflict,
O, Maria, in dein Herz.	Mary, on thy heart !
Ach, dein Sohn muss dich verlassen	Ah, thy Son must leave thee now
Um am Kreuze zu erblassen,	On the cross to faint, to die ;—
Wer ermisst den Mutterschmerz ?	Who can weigh that Mother's woe ?

FIRST TABLEAU.—THE DEPARTURE OF TOBIAS FROM HIS HOME.

Chorus.

Freunde, welch'ein herber Schmerz	What a bitter grief, O friends,
Folterte das Mutterherz,	Agonized the mother's heart,
Als Tobias an der Hand	As Tobias,—Raphael
Raphaels in fremdes Land	His guide,—at his father's word
Auf Befehl des Vater's eilte !	Hastened to a foreign land !
Unter tausend Weh'und Ach	With a thousand woes and sighs
Ruft sie dem Geliebten nach :	Oft on her beloved she calls :
Komme, ach, verweile nicht,	" Come, ah, come, and tarry not,
Meines Herzens Trost und Licht !	Light and comfort of my heart,
Komme, komme bald zurücke !	Come, return full soon again !
Ach, Tobias ! Theuerster !	Ah, Tobias, dearest one !
Eil' in meine Arme her,	Haste thee to mine arms again,
Liebster Sohn ! an dir allein	Dearest son ! in thee alone
Wird mein Herz sich wieder freu'n.	Can my heart again rejoice—
Freuen sich der schönsten Freude.	Joy in fairest happiness.
Trostlos jammert sie nun so,	Comfortless it now laments,
Nimmer ihres Lebens froh,	Never of existence glad,
Bis ein sel'ger Augenblick	Till a bright and blissful hour
In den Mutterschooss zurück	To his mother's breast once more
Den geliebten Sohn wird führen.	Her beloved son shall bring."

SECOND TABLEAU.—THE LAMENTING BRIDE OF THE CANTICLES, WITH EIGHT DAUGHTERS OF JERUSALEM.

Chorus.

Wo ist er hin? Wo ist er hin	Whither is he gone, O whither ?
Der Schöne aller Schönen ?	Fairest of the sons of men !
Mein Auge weinet, ach ! um ihn	Ah, mine eyes run down with tears—
Der Liebe heisse Thränen.	Tears of tender love for him.
Ach, komme doch ! ach, komme doch !	Come, O come, return again !
Sieh diese Thränen fliessen :	See my ever-flowing tears :
Geliebter ! wie ? Du zögerst noch	What, belov'd ! thou dost delay
Dich an mein Herz zu schliessen?	Me to thy dear heart to clasp ?
Mein Auge forschet überall	Everywhere I look for thee,
Nach Dir auf allen Wegen :	Seek for thee in every place,
Und mit der Sonne erstem Strahl	With the sun's first ray of light
Eilt Dir mein Herz entgegen.	Hastes my heart to meet thy steps.
Geliebter ! ach ! was fühle ich ?	Ah ! what feel I ! my beloved !
Wie ist mein Herz beklommen !	With what anguish breaks my heart !

Chorus of Daughters of Jerusalem.

Geliebte Freundin ! tröste Dich ; Dein Freund wird wieder kommen.	Beloved companion, comfort take ! Thy friend again will come to thee.
O harre Freundin ! bald kommt er, Schlingt sich an Deine Seite ; Dann trübet keine Wolke mehr Des Wiedersehens Freude.	O wait, dear maid, he quickly comes, And clasps thee to his heart again :— No cloud can ever darken more The bliss of that re-union.

Both Choruses.

O komm' in meine Arme her, Schling Dich an meine Seite ; Und keine Wolke trübe mehr Des Wiedersehens Freude.	O come into mine arms, O come ! And clasp me to thy heart again ; And no cloud ever darken more The bliss of that re-union !

SCENE I.

CHRIST *and the Twelve* DISCIPLES.

Christ. Ye know, beloved disciples, that after two days is the feast of the Passover. Let us then now take our last rest with our friends at Bethany, and then go up to Jerusalem, where in these days all will be fulfilled which is written in the Prophets concerning the Son of man.

Philip. Has the day then come at last when Thou wilt restore again the kingdom to Israel ?

Christ. The Son of man shall be delivered up to the Gentiles, and shall be mocked and spitted upon, and they shall crucify Him, but on the third day He shall rise again.

John. Master, what dark, fearful words speakest Thou ! How shall these things come to pass ? Tell us plainly.

Christ. The hour is come that the Son of man should be glorified. Verily, verily, I say unto you, except a corn of wheat fall into the ground and die, it abideth alone : but if it die, it bringeth forth much fruit. Now is the judgment of this world : now shall the prince of this world be cast out. And I, if I be lifted up from the earth, will draw all men unto me.

Thaddæus. What meaneth He by these words ?

Simon. Wherefore doth He liken Himself to a corn of wheat ?

Andrew. Lord, Thou speakest at once of shame and of victory. I know not how to reconcile these in my thoughts.

Christ. That which is dark as night to you will become clear as day. I have told you before that ye may not lose courage whatever may happen. Believe and hope. When the tribulation is over then shall ye see and understand.

Thomas. I cannot consent to that which Thou speakest of suffering and of death. What can Thine enemies do to Thee ? One single word from Thee will grind them to powder.

Christ. Thomas, adore the secret counsel of God which thou canst not fathom. Yet a little while is the light with you. Walk while ye have the light, lest darkness come upon you.

SCENE II.

Enter SIMON, LAZARUS, MARTHA, *and* MARY MAGDALENE.

Simon. Dearest Master, I greet Thee.

Christ. Simon, for the last time I, with my disciples, claim thy hospitality.

Simon. Not so, Lord. Often again shall Bethany secure to Thee a short repose.

Christ. Lo, Lazarus, our friend !

Lazarus (embracing Him). My Lord, conqueror of death !

Magdalene. Rabbi !

Martha, Hail, Rabbi !

Christ. The blessing of God be upon you !

Martha. Shall I dare, O Lord, to serve Thee ?

Magdalene. Wilt Thou also not despise a token of love from me ?

Christ. Do that which is in your heart to do, dear souls.

Simon. Dearest Master, enter under my roof and refresh Thyself and Thy disciples.

SCENE III.

The Guest-chamber in SIMON'S *House.* (*See* p. 11.)

Christ. Peace be to this house !

Disciples. And to all who dwell therein !

Simon. Lord, all is prepared.

Christ. Let us then, beloved disciples, with thankfulness enjoy the gifts which the Father from heaven vouchsafes to us through His servant Simon. O Jerusalem ! O that my coming were as dear to thee as it is to these my friends ! But thou art stricken with blindness.

Lazarus. Yea, Lord, the Pharisees and teachers of the law watch for Thy destruction.

Simon. Tarry here ; here Thou art in safety.

Peter. Lord, it is good to be here. Tarry here till the storm which will gather has broken.

Christ. Get thee behind me, tempter ! Thou savourest not the things that be of God, but those that be of men. Shall the reaper tarry in the shade when the fields are ripe unto harvest ? The Son of man came not to be ministered unto, but to minister, and to give His life a ransom for many.

Judas. But, Lord, what will become of us when Thou givest up Thy life?

An Apostle. Alas! all our hopes have, then, come to nothing.

Christ. Calm yourselves. I have power to lay down my life, and I have power to take it again. This commandment have I received of my Father.

Magdalene (*advances and pours ointment upon the head of* CHRIST). Rabbi!

Christ. Mary!

Thomas. What a costly odour!

Bartholomew. It is a costly precious ointment of spikenard.

Judas. To what purpose is this waste? The cost of it might have been better laid out.

Thomas. To me also it seemeth thus.

[MAGDALENE *kneels and anoints the feet of* CHRIST.

Judas. To pour away such a costly ointment! What waste!

Christ. Friend Judas, look me in the face! Waste on Me, on thy Master?

Judas. I know that Thou lovest not useless expense. The ointment might have been sold and the poor thereby supported.

Christ. Judas, lay thy hand upon thy heart. Is it only sympathy for the poor which so greatly moves thee?

Judas. Three hundred pence at least could have been got for it. What a loss for the poor and for us!

Christ. The poor ye have always with you, but me ye have not always. Let her alone, she hath wrought a good work on me, for in that she poured this ointment on me she did it for my burial. Verily I say unto you: wheresoever this Gospel shall be preached through the whole world there shall also that which she hath done be told for a memorial of her. (*To* SIMON) I thank thee, thou beneficent one, for thy hospitality. The Father will reward thee for it.

Simon. Master, speak not of thanks. I know what I owe to Thee.

Christ. It is time to go hence. Farewell to all, O dwellers in this hospitable house! Follow me, my disciples.

Peter. Lord, whithersoever Thou willest, only not to Jerusalem.

Christ. I go whither my Father calls me. Peter, if it please thee to remain here, do so.

Peter. Lord, where Thou abidest, there also will I abide, where Thou goest, there also will I go.

Christ. Come, then!

SCENE IV.

Christ (to MAGDALENE *and* MARTHA). Tarry here, beloved! Once more, farewell! Beloved, peaceful Bethany! Never more shall I tarry amid thy still valleys.

Simon. Master, wilt Thou then indeed depart hence? Ah, fearful forebodings oppress me!

Christ. Stand up, Mary! The night cometh, and the storms of winter howl around! Yet—be comforted! In the early morning in the spring-garden thou shalt see me again.

Martha. Alas! dost Thou depart and never more return?

Christ. The Father wills it, my loved ones! Where I am I bear you in my heart, and where ye are there will my blessing follow you. Farewell!   [*As He is going,* MARY *enters with her companions.*

SCENE V.

Mary. Jesus, most dear Son, with desire have I hastened to Thee with my friends to see Thee again before, alas! Thou goest hence.

Christ. Mother! I am on the way to Jerusalem.

Mary. To Jerusalem! There is the Temple of Jehovah, whither once I bore Thee in my arms, to offer Thee to the Lord.

Christ. Mother, now has the hour come when I, according to the Father's will, shall offer Myself. I am ready to accomplish the sacrifice which the Father requires from me.

Mary. Ah, forebodings tell me what an offering this will be!

Magdalene. O, how greatly have we longed to keep back the Master with us!

Simon. His resolve is steadfast.

Christ. Mine hour is come. Now is my soul troubled, and what shall I say: Father, save me from this hour? But for this hour came I into the world.

Mary. O Simeon, venerable old man! now will that which thou didst prophesy to me be fulfilled: "A sword shall pierce through thine own soul."

Christ. Mother! the Father's will was ever sacred to thee also.

Mary. It is so to me. I am the handmaid of the Lord. Only for one thing, my Son, I pray Thee.

Christ. What desirest thou, my Mother?

Mary. That I may die with Thee.

John. What love!

Christ. Thou wilt suffer with me, beloved Mother, thou wilt combat with me, and then also rejoice with me in my victory. Therefore be comforted !

Mary. O God, give me strength !

Holy Women. Dearest Mother, we weep with thee.

Mary. I go then with Thee, my Son, to Jerusalem.

Women. Dearest Mother, we go with thee.

Christ. Later ye may go thither ; but now abide with our friends at Bethany. I commend to you, O faithful souls, my beloved Mother, with those who have followed her thither.

Magdalene. There is none dearer to us after Thee than Thy Mother.

Lazarus. If Thou, O Master, couldst but tarry !

Christ. Comfort ye one another ! But after two days ye may together take your way to Jerusalem in order to be there upon the great day of the feast.

Mary. As Thou willest, my Son.

Women. Alas, how sadly will the hours pass by far from Thee !

Christ. Mother ! Mother ! For the tender love and Motherly care which thou hast shown to me during the thirty-three years of my life receive the warmest gratitude of thy Son. The Father calls me. Farewell, dearest, dearest Mother !

Mary. My Son, where shall I see Thee again ?

Christ. There, dearest Mother, where the Scripture shall be fulfilled : He was led as a lamb to the slaughter, and He opened not His mouth.

All. What affliction is before us all !

Christ. Be not overcome in the first struggle ! Hold ye still in me.

[Exit.

ACT IV.

CHRIST'S LAST JOURNEY TO JERUSALEM. (*See* p. 12.)

PROLOGUE.

People of God ! behold, thy Redeemer is at hand. The long promised One has come. O hear Him ! Follow His leading. Life and blessing will He bring thee, yet Jerusalem shows herself deaf and blind, and puts back the offered hand. Therefore the Highest turns away from her, and lets her sink into perdition. The pride of Vashti disdains the King's banquet, therefore the King, grievously provoked, banishes her from His Presence, and chooses a nobler soul as His consort. Thus will the synagogue be cast out, and the kingdom of God, taken from it, will be given to other nations, which shall bring forth the fruits of righteousness.

E

Chorus.

Jerusalem ! Jerusalem ! erwache !
Erkenne, was zum Frieden dir noch
 werden kann
Doch zögerst du—so fängt die Zeit der
 Rache,
Unselige ! mit fürchterlichen Schlägen an.

Awake, Jerusalem, awake !
And know what yet belongeth to thy
 peace :
But waverest thou—the hour of vengeance
 comes,
Unhappy one ! with awful sound it strikes.

Jerusalem ! Jerusalem !
 Bekehre dich zu deinem Gott !
Verachte nicht mit Frevelspott
 Den Mahnungsruf der Gnade,
Dass nicht, Unselige, über dich
Dereinst in vollen Schalen sich
 Des Höchsten Grimm entlade !

Jerusalem ! Jerusalem !
 Return thee to thy God !
Scorn not, with evil mockery,
 The warning call of grace ;
That not, unhappy one, on thee
In measure full one day be poured
 The anger of our God most High !

Doch, ach !—ach ! die Propheten-Mör-
 derin—
Sie taumelt fort in ihrem bösen Sinn.
 Darum, so spricht der Herr,
 Diess Volk will ich nicht mehr.

But ah,—alas ! the prophet-murd'ress,

With evil mind she rushes on.
 Therefore, thus saith the Lord,
 This people I reject.

TABLEAU.—VASHTI REJECTED BY AHASUERUS, AND ESTHER CHOSEN QUEEN.

Chorus.

Seht Vasthi—seht ! die Stolze wird verstossen !
Ein Bild, was mit der Synagog der Herr
 beschlossen.

See Vashti—see the proud one is cast out !

Figuring God's purpose for the Synagogue.

Entferne dich von meinem Throne,
Du stolzes Weib ! unwerth der Krone ;
 So spricht Assuerus ganz ergrimmt.
Dir, schöne Esther ! dir sei heute
Zu herrschen an des Könige Seite
 Hier dieser Königsthron bestimmt.

" Remove thee now from off my throne,
Proud Queen ! deserving not the crown,"
 Ahasuerus speaks in wrath.
" Thine, fairest Esther, thine it is
This day beside the King to reign,
 Here chosen for the royal throne."

Die Zeit der Gnade ist verflossen ;
Diess stolze Volk will ich verstossen,
 So wahr ich lebe, spricht der Herr.
Ein besser Volk wird er sich wählen,
Mit ihm auf ewig sich vermählen,
 Wie mit der Esther Assuer.

" The time of grace hath pass'd away ;
I will cast out this nation proud,
 Even as I live," thus saith the Lord.
" A better people I will choose—
Espouse to me for ever more,
 As Esther Ahasuerus chose."

Jerusalem ! Jerusalem !
Ihr Sünder ! höret Gottes Wort !
 Wollt ihr noch Gnade finden,
So schafft aus eu'ren Herzen fort
 Den Sauerteig der Sünden.

Jerusalem ! Jerusalem !
Ye sinners ! hear the word of God.
 Even still would ye find grace.
Destroy from out your inmost hearts
 The leaven of your sins.

SCENE I.

CHRIST *and the Twelve on the Way to Jerusalem.*

John. Master, behold what a splendid outlook towards Jerusalem!

Matthew. And the majestic Temple. What a stately building!

Christ. Jerusalem, Jerusalem! O that thou hadst known even in this thy day, the things that belong unto thy peace! But now they are hid from thine eyes. (*He weeps.*)

Peter. Master, wherefore grievest thou so sorely?

Christ. My Peter! the fate of this unhappy city goes to my heart.

John. Master, tell us, what will be this fate?

Christ. The days will come when her enemies shall make a trench about her, and close her in on every side, and they shall lay her even with the ground, and her children in her; and they shall not leave one stone upon another.

Andrew. Wherefore shall the city have so sad a fate?

Christ. Because she hath not known the day of her visitation. Alas! the murderers of the Prophets will kill the Messiah Himself.

All. What a fearful deed!

James the Great. God forbid that the city of God should lay such a curse upon itself!

John. Master, for the holy city's sake, for the Temple's sake, I pray Thee go not thither, so that the opportunity may be wanting to evil men to accomplish the worst.

Peter. Or go thither, and manifest Thyself to them in Thy full majesty, that the good may rejoice, and the evil tremble.

Philip. Strike down Thine enemies!

All. And set up the kingdom of God amongst men!

Christ. Children, what ye desire will come to pass in its time, but my ways are appointed unto me before of my Father, and thus saith the Lord: My thoughts are not your thoughts, neither are my ways your ways. To-day is the first day of unleavened bread, on which the law commands that the paschal meal shall be held. Do ye both, Peter and John, go before, and prepare us the paschal lamb, that we may eat it in the evening.

Peter and John. Where wilt Thou, Lord, that we should prepare it?

Christ. When ye shall come unto the city, there shall a man meet you bearing a pitcher of water; follow him into the house whither he goeth, and say to the master of the house: The Master saith unto thee, where is the guest-chamber where I shall eat the passover with my disciples? And he will show you a large upper room, furnished and prepared; there make it ready.

Peter. Thy blessing, dearest Master. (PETER *and* JOHN *kneel.*)

Christ. God's blessing be upon you! [*Exeunt the two Apostles.*

E 2

Scene II.

Christ. And ye—follow me for the last time to my Father's house! To-day ye still go thither with me. To-morrow——

Judas. But, Master, let me say, if in truth Thou wilt leave us, make at least some arrangement for our future sustenance. See here (*he shows the bag*), this is not sufficient for one day more.

Christ. Judas, be not more careful than is needful.

Judas. How well might the worth of that ointment be therein! Three hundred pence! How long we might have lived without anxiety!

Christ. Nothing has ever been wanting to thee, and, believe me, nothing will at any time be wanting to thee.

Judas. Yet, Master, when Thou art no longer with us our good friends will soon draw back, and then——

Christ. Friend Judas, see to it, that the tempter overtake thee not!

All. Judas, trouble not then the Master so sorely.

Judas. Who will take thought if I do not? Have I not been appointed by the Master to carry the bag?

Christ. That thou art, but I fear——

Judas. I also fear that it will soon be empty, and will remain so.

Christ. Judas, forget not my warning! Now let us go on. I long to be in my Father's house.

[*Exit with the Disciples.* Judas *remains behind.*

Scene III.

Judas *alone.*

Wherefore should I follow Him? I have no pleasure therein. The Master's behaviour is to me inexplicable. His great works give hope that He will again raise up the kingdom of Israel. But He seizes not the opportunities which offer themselves, and now He speaks of separation and death, and comforts us by mysterious words about a dim future. I am weary of believing and of hoping.   There is nothing in prospect with Him, except approaching poverty and humiliation, and, instead of the expected participation in His kingdom, persecution, perchance, and prison. I will withdraw myself. Happily, I was always provident, and have laid aside a little here and there out of the bag, on the chance of distress. If that fool had put the worth of the ointment into the bag, now, when our company must, as it seems, break up, the three hundred pence would remain in my hands, then I should be secure for a long time. Now, however, I must think of means by which I may be able to make some profit.

SCENE IV.

JUDAS *and the Trader* DATHAN.

Dathan (aside). Judas—the occasion is favourable, he is alone, he seems much perplexed. I must use all means to win him. Friend Judas!

Judas. Who calls?

Dathan. A friend. Has something sad happened to thee? Thou art so deep in thought.

Judas. Who art thou?

Dathan. Thy friend, thy brother.

Judas. Thou?

Dathan. At least I wish to become so.· How is it with the Master? I also might enter His Society.

Judas. His Society? . . . . .

Dathan. Hast thou perchance left Him? Is it ill with Him? Tell me, that I may rule myself accordingly.

Judas. If thou canst be silent——

Dathan. Be assured of it.

Judas. Things no longer go well with Him. He says it Himself, that His last hour is come. I will leave Him. I have charge of the bag— look and see how things are here.

Dathan. Friend, then I remain as I am.

SCENE V.

DATHAN'S *Companions steal in.*

Judas. Who are these? I will say no more.

Traders. Stay, friend, you will not rue it.

Judas. Wherefore have ye come hither?

Traders. We desire to return to Jerusalem and bear thee company, if it please thee.

Judas. Will ye perchance go after the Master?

Traders. Has He gone to Jerusalem?

Judas. For the last time, as He says.

Traders. Will he then leave Judæa?

Judas. Why ask ye so eagerly? Will ye become His followers?

Traders. Wherefore not, if favourable prospects are in that quarter?

Judas. I see nothing of that sort. He ever says to us, take no thought for the morrow—but if to-day any mischances befall Him there we are all beggars. Doth a master care thus for his own?

Traders. Truly the outlook is bad enough.

Judas (relates the story of the ointment).

Traders. And thou canst yet be friends with Him? Thou oughtest to take thought for thine own future, were it only now.

Judas. I am thinking of it even now. But how to find a good livelihood at once?

Dathan. Thou needest not long seek that; the fairest opportunity offers itself.

Judas. Where—how?

Traders. Hast thou heard nothing of the proclamation of the High Priest's Council? A fairer opportunity thou wilt not in thy whole life again find.

Judas. What proclamation?

Traders. Whosoever informs concerning the nightly resort of Jesus of Nazareth will receive a large reward.

Judas. A large reward!

Traders. Who can deserve it easier than thou?

Dathan (*aside*). We are near our aim.

Traders. Brother, trifle not with thy fortune.

Judas (*aside*). A fair opportunity—shall I let it slip from my hands?

Dathan. And consider: the reward is not all. The Council will take further thought for thee. Who knows what thou mayest become?

Traders. Make up your mind, friend!

Judas. Well, so be it!

Dathan. Come, Judas, we will bring thee at once to the Council.

Judas. Just now I must go after the Master. I will first get information in order to act more securely. Report me beforehand to the Council. In three hours you will find me in the street of the Temple.

Dathan. Brother, one word——

Judas. A Man!   [*Exeunt the* TRADERS.

SCENE VI.

JUDAS *alone.* (*See* p. 13.)

My word is given. I shall not rue it. Shall I, forsooth, go out of the way of this approaching good fortune? Yes, my future is made. I will do what I have promised; let me, however, reckon things up beforehand. If the Priests succeed in taking Him Prisoner, then shall I have brought my net to land, and shall besides become famous, as one who has helped to save the law of Moses. But if the Master conquers . . . then will I cast myself repentant at His feet. He is indeed good; never have I seen Him cast a penitent away from Him. He will receive me again, and then I shall have the merit of having brought things to a decision. Judas, thou art a prudent man . . . yet I am afraid to come before the Master. I shall not be able to bear His piercing glance, and my companions will see in my face that I am a —— No! that I will not be, I am no traitor! What am I doing except showing the Jews where the Master is to be found? That is no betrayal; more is needed for that. Away with these fancies! Courage, Judas, thy livelihood is at stake!

ACT V.

THE LAST SUPPER. (*See* p. 13.)

PROLOGUE.

Before the Divine Friend, constrained by love, departs to His Passion, He gives Himself to His own as Food of the soul during their earthly pilgrimage. Ready to offer Himself, He consecrates a sacrificial Banquet, which, through a thousand years and on to the close of time, shall proclaim His love to rescued humanity. Once with manna in the wilderness the Lord mercifully satisfied the children of Israel, and made glad their hearts with clusters of grapes from Canaan. But a better Feast, from Heaven itself, doth Jesus offer us. From the mystery of His Body and Blood flow grace and blessedness to us.

Chorus.

Nun nähert sich die Stunde,
  Und die Erfüllung fängt sich an,
Was längst in der Propheten Munde
  Der Herr der Menschheit kund gethan.

The hour now draweth near,
  Fulfilment now begins
Of all which by His seers
  God to mankind made known.

An diesem Volke, spricht der Herr,
Hab' ich kein Wohlgefallen mehr ;
  Ich will nun keine Opfergaben
  Von seinen Händen ferner haben.

" In this folk," saith the Lord,
" Have I no pleasure more,
  And sacrifice will I
  No more from them receive.

Ich stifte mir ein neues Mahl :
Diess spricht der Herr :—und überall
  Soll auf dem ganzen Erdenrunde
  Ein Opfer sein in diesem Bunde.

A new feast I establish,"
Thus saith the Lord ; " and it shall be
  Throughout the world's great circle
  An off'ring of this covenant."

FIRST TABLEAU.—THE MANNA IN THE WILDERNESS.

Chorus.

Das Wunder in der Wüste Sin
Zeigt auf das Mahl des neuen Bundes hin.

The miracle in the desert Sin
Points to the second covenant's Feast.

Gut ist der Herr, gut ist der Herr :
Das Volk das hungert, sättigt er
  Mit einer neuen Speise
  Auf wunderbare Weise.

Good is the Lord, the Lord is good !
He satisfies the hungry souls
  With a new Food
  In wondrous wise.

Der Tod doch raffte alle hin,
Die assen in der Wüste Sin
  Diess Brod im Ueberflusse ;
Des neuen Bundes heilig Brod
Bewahrt die Seele vor dem Tod
  Beim würdigen Genusse.

But death all those hath swept away,
Who in the wilderness of Sin
  Did eat in fulness of that bread ;
The second covenant's holy Bread
Spirit and soul preserves from death
  When worthily enjoyed.

SECOND TABLEAU.—THE GRAPES BROUGHT BY THE SPIES FROM CANAAN.

Chorus.

Gut ist der Herr, gut ist der Herr !
Dem Volke einstens hatte er
   Den besten Saft der Reben
   Aus Kanaan gegeben.

Doch diess Gewächse der Natur
War zum Bedarf des Leibes nur
   Bestimmt nach Gottes Willen.
Des neuen Bundes heil'ger Wein
Wird selbst das Blut des Sohnes sein,
   Der Seele Durst zu stillen.

Gut ist der Herr, gut ist der Herr,
Im neuen Bunde reichet er
   Sein Fleisch und Blut im Saale
   Zu Salem bei dem Mahle.

Good is the Lord, the Lord is good
Once hath He to His people
   The best juice of the vine
   Given from Canaan's land.

Yet this, the growth of Nature
For needs of body only,
   By God's Will was designed.
The second cov'nant's holy wine
Will be itself the Son's own blood—
   Thirst of the soul to quench.

The Lord is good, the Lord is good
In the new covenant He gives
   His Flesh and Blood at that high Feast
   In Salem's upper room.

SCENE I. (*See* pp. 13, 14.)

The Upper Chamber. CHRIST *and the Twelve at the Table.*

Christ. With desire I have desired to eat this Passover with you before I suffer. For I say unto you, I will not any more eat thereof until it be fulfilled in the kingdom of God. Father, I thank Thee for this fruit of the vine. (*He drinks and gives the cup to the* DISCIPLES.) Take this and divide it among yourselves ; for I say unto you, I will not drink henceforth of the fruit of the vine until the kingdom of God shall come.

Apostles. Alas! Lord, is this, then, the last Passover ?

Christ. There is a cup which I will drink with you in the kingdom of God, as it is written : Thou shalt make them drink of the river of Thy pleasures.

Peter. Master, when this kingdom shall appear, how then shall the places be portioned out ?

James the Great. Which of us shall have the first place ?

Christ. So long a time have I been with you, and ye are yet entangled in that which is of the earth ! Verily, I appoint unto you which have continued with me in my temptations a kingdom, as my Father hath appointed unto me, that ye may eat and drink with me at my table in my kingdom, and sit on thrones judging the twelve tribes of Israel. But consider well : the kings of the Gentiles exercise lordship over them, and they that exercise authority upon them are called benefactors. But it shall not be so among you ; but he that is greatest among you let him be as the younger, and he that is chief as he that doth serve. For whether is greater he that sitteth at meat, or he that serveth? Is not he that sitteth at meat? But I am among you as he that serveth. (*He lays aside His garment, girds himself with a white towel, and pours water into a basin.*) Now sit down, beloved disciples!

Apostles. What will He do?

Christ. Peter, give me thy foot!

Peter. Lord, dost Thou wash my feet?

Christ. What I do thou knowest not now; but thou shalt know hereafter.

Peter. Lord, Thou shalt never wash my feet!

Christ. If I wash thee not thou hast no part with me.

Peter. Lord, if it be so, not my feet only, but also my hands and my head.

Christ. He that is washed needeth not save to wash his feet, but is clean every whit. (*He washes all the* DISCIPLES' *feet. After He has taken His garment again He stands looking round upon the circle.*) Ye are now clean—but not all! (*He sits down.*) Know ye what I have done to you? Ye call me Master and Lord: and ye say well, for so I am. If I, then, your Lord and Master, have washed your feet, ye also ought to wash one another's feet! For I have given you an example that ye should do as I have done to you. Verily, verily, I say unto you, the servant is not greater than he that sent him. If ye know these things, happy are ye if ye do them. (*He stands up.*) Children! but for a little while longer shall I be with you. That my remembrance may never perish from amongst you I will leave you an everlasting memorial, and so ever dwell with you and amongst you. The old covenant which my Father made with Abraham, Isaac, and Jacob hath reached its end. And I say unto you: a new covenant begins, which I solemnly consecrate to-day in my blood, as the Father hath given the commandment—and this covenant will last till all be fulfilled. (*He takes bread, blesses, and breaks it.*) Take, eat; this is my Body, which is given for you. (*He gives a small portion to each of the* DISCIPLES.) This do in remembrance of me. (*He takes the cup with wine and blesses it.*) Take this, and drink ye all of it; for this is the cup of the New Testament in my blood, which is shed for you and for many for the remission of sins. (*He gives the cup to all.*) As often as ye do this, do it in remembrance of me. (*He sits down.*)

John. Dearest Master, never will I forget Thy love! Thou knowest that I love Thee! (*He leans on* JESUS' *breast.*)

Apostles. O! most loving One, ever will we remain united to Thee!

Peter. This holy supper of the new covenant shall ever be set forth amongst us according to Thine ordinance.

All. Most beloved Teacher!

Christ. My children, abide in me, and I in you. As the Father hath loved me, so have I loved you. Continue ye in my love. But, alas!—

must I say it ?—the hand of him that betrayeth me is with me on the table !

Several Apostles. What !—a betrayer amongst us ?

Peter. Is it possible ?

Christ. Verily, verily, I say unto you, one of you shall betray me !

Andrew. Lord, one of us twelve ?

Christ. Yea, one of the twelve !　One who dippeth his hand with me in the dish shall betray me.　The Scripture will be fulfilled : he that eateth bread with me hath lifted up his heel against me.

Thomas and Simon. Who shall this faithless one be ?

The two Jameses. Name him openly, the infamous one !

Judas. Lord, is it I ?

Thaddæus. Rather my life for Thee than such an act !

Christ (to JUDAS). Thou hast said.　(*To all.*) The Son of man indeed goeth as it is written of Him ; but woe unto that man by whom the Son of man is betrayed !　Good were it for that man if he had never been born !

Peter (whispers to JOHN). Who is it of whom He speaks ?

John (whispers to JESUS). Lord, who is it ?

Christ (whispers to JOHN). He it is to whom I shall give a sop when I have dipped it.

Several Apostles. Who can it then be ?　　　　　　'

Christ (after He has given the sop to JUDAS). That thou doest do quickly.　　　　　　　　　　　　[JUDAS *hastens out of the room.*

Thomas (to SIMON). Wherefore goeth Judas away ?

Simon. Probably the Master sends him to buy somewhat.

Thaddæus. Or to give alms to the poor.

SCENE II.

Christ. Now is the Son of man glorified, and God is glorified in Him. If God be glorified in Him God shall also glorify Him in Himself, and shall straightway glorify Him.　Little children, yet a little while I am with you.　Ye shall seek me ; and as I said unto the Jews, Whither I go, ye cannot come ; so now I say to you.

Peter. Lord, whither goest thou ?

Christ. Whither I go thou canst not follow me now.

Peter. Why cannot I follow Thee now ?　I will lay down my life for Thy sake.

Christ. Wilt thou lay down thy life for my sake ?　Simon, Simon ! Satan hath desired to have you, that he may sift you as wheat.　But I have prayed for thee, that thy faith fail not ; and when thou art converted, strengthen thy brethren.　All ye shall be offended because of me this night, for it is written: I will smite the Shepherd, and the sheep of the flock shall be scattered abroad.

Peter. Although all shall be offended, yet will not I. Lord, I am ready to go with Thee both into prison and to death.

Christ. Verily, verily, I tell thee, Peter, that this day, even in this night, before the cock crow twice, thou shalt deny me thrice.

Peter. If I should die with Thee I will not deny Thee in anywise.

All. Master, we also will remain ever true to Thee! None of us will at any time deny Thee.

Christ. When I sent you without purse, and scrip, and shoes, lacked ye anything?

All. No! Nothing.

Christ. But now, he that hath a purse, let him take it, and likewise his scrip; and he that hath no sword, let him sell his garment and buy one. For the time of trial is beginning, and I say unto you that this that is written must yet be accomplished in me: And He was reckoned among the transgressors.

Peter and Philip. Lord, behold here are two swords.

Christ. It is enough. Let us stand up and say the prayer of thanksgiving. (*With the* DISCIPLES.) Praise the Lord, all ye people! Praise Him, all ye nations! For His merciful kindness is ever more and more towards us, and the truth of the Lord endureth for ever! (*He advances to the foreground and stands there awhile with His eyes raised to heaven. The* APOSTLES *stand on either side sorrowful and gazing at Him.*) Children, why are ye so sad, and why look ye on me so sorrowfully? Let not your heart be troubled; ye believe in God, believe also in me. In my Father's house are many mansions; I go to prepare a place for you, and I will come again and receive you unto myself, that where I am there ye may be also. I leave you not as orphans. Peace I leave with you; my peace I give unto you: not as the world giveth give I unto you. Keep my commandment! This is my commandment: That ye love one another as I have loved you. By this shall all men know that ye are my disciples, if ye have love one to another. Hereafter, I will not talk much with you, for the Prince of this world cometh, although he hath nothing in me. But that the world may know that I love the Father, and as the Father gave the commandment, even so I do. [*Exeunt.*

ACT VI.

THE BETRAYAL. (*See* p. 14.)

PROLOGUE.

Alas, the false friend joins himself to the open enemies, and a few pieces of silver destroy all love and truth in the heart of the fool! Remorseless, this most thankless one departs, to conclude a shameful bargaining in life; the best of Teachers is put up to sale by him for a contemptible traitor's reward. The like disposition hardened Jacob's sons so that they pitilessly sold their own brother for an accursed price to strange usurers. Where the heart worships the idol of gold there all nobler dispositions are killed; honour, and man's word, and love and friendship become saleable.

Chorus.

Wie schaudert's mir durch alle Glieder!	What shudders run through all my limbs!
Wohin? wohin, o Judas! voller Wuth?	Where go'st thou, Judas, full of rage?
Bist du der Schurke, der das Blut	Art thou the villain, who the Blood
Verkaufen wird? Gerechte Rache, säume nicht—	Wilt sell? Just Vengeance, tarry not—
Ihr Donner—Blitze stürzet nieder—	Ye thunders—Lightnings cast him down—
Zermalmet diesen Bösewicht!	Crush, rend this wretch in pieces.
Von Euch wird Einer mich verrathen!	" One amongst you shall Me betray!"
Und dreimal sprach der Herr diess Wort.	Three times this word the Master spake.
Vom Geiz verführt zu schwarzen Thaten,	By greed seduced to blackest deed
Lief einer von dem Mahle fort;	One from the Supper quickly went;
Und dieser Eine—heil'ger Gott!—	And this one—O thou holy God!—
Ist Judas, der Iskariot.	Is Judas, the Iscariot.
Ach Judas! Judas—welche Sünde!—	O Judas, Judas! what a crime!
Vollende nicht die schwarze That!	Complete not, O, that darkest deed!
Doch nein—vom Geize taub und blinde,	But no—by greed made deaf and blind,
Eilt Judas fort zum hohen Rath.	To the Sanhedrim Judas hastes;
Und wiederholt voll bösem Sinn	With wicked heart he now repeats
Was einst geschah zu Dothain.	What once was done in Dothan's field.

TABLEAU.—JOSEPH SOLD BY HIS BRETHREN TO THE ISHMAELITES.

Chorus.

" Was bietet für den Knaben ihr?—	" What will ye offer for the lad?—
So sprechen, Brüder, wenn euch wir Ihn käuflich übergeben?"	Answer us, brothers,—if we now Deliver him for gold?"
Sie geben bald um den Gewinn	They quickly give for the poor gain
Von zwanzig Silberlingen hin	Of twenty silver pieces told,
Des Bruders Blut und Leben.	Their brother's blood and life.

" Was gebet ihr?—wie lohnt ihr mich?"	" What give ye? how reward ye me?"
Spricht der Iskariot, " wenn ich	The Iscariot says, "if I
Den Meister euch verrathe?"	My Lord betray to you?"
Um dreissig Silberlinge schliesst	For thirty silver coins he makes
Den Blutbund er, und Jesus ist	The bloody bargain :—Jesus is
Verkauft dem hohen Rathe.	To the Sandedrim sold.
Was diese Scene uns vorhält,	What this sad scene to us sets forth
Ist ein getreues Bild der Welt.	Of this world is an image true.
Wie oft habt ihr durch eure Thaten	How often have ye by your deeds
Auch euren Gott verkauft—verrathen!	Your God e'en thus betray'd and sold?
Den Brüdern eines Joseph hier,	On Joseph's brethren ye pour
Und einem Judas fluchet ihr,	Curses, and on th' Iscariot,
Und wandelt doch auf ihren Wegen ;	And yet in the same paths ye tread ;
Denn Neid und Geiz und Bruderhass	For envy, greed, and brother's hate
Zerstören ohne Unterlass	Unceasingly exterminate
Der Menschheit Frieden, Glück und Segen.	Man's peace, and joy, and blessedness.

SCENE I.

The Sanhedrim.

Caiaphas. Assembled Fathers, I have joyful news to impart to you. The supposed Prophet of Galilee will soon, we hope, be in our hands. Dathan, the zealous Israelite, has won over one of the most trusted followers of the Galilæan, who consents to be employed as guide for the night attack. Both are ready here, and only await our summons (*he sends a Priest to bring in* DATHAN *and* JUDAS). Now, however, I must take your advice as to the price which should be given for the deed.

Nathanael. The law of Moses instructs us concerning it. A slave is reckoned at thirty pieces of silver.

A Priest. Yes, yes, such a price for a slave is the worth of the false Messiah.

SCENE II.

DATHAN *and* JUDAS before the *Sanhedrim.* (*See p.* 15.)

Dathan. Most learned Council, here is the man who is determined for a suitable reward to deliver your and our Enemy.

Caiaphas (*to* JUDAS). Knowest thou the man whom the Council seeks ?

Judas. I have been in His company now for a long time and know Him ; and I know where He is wont to abide.

Caiaphas. What is thy name ?

Judas. I am called JUDAS, and am one of the Twelve.

Priests. Yes, yes, we often saw thee with Him.

Caiaphas. Art thou now steadfastly resolved to do after our will ?

Judas. Thereto I give thee my word.

Caiaphas. Wilt thou not repent of it ?

Judas. The friendship between Him and me has for some time cooled, and now I have quite broken with Him.

Caiaphas. What has prompted thee to this ?

Judas. It is no longer with Him . . . and . . . I am resolved to submit myself to lawful authority ; that is always the best. What will ye give me if I deliver Him unto you ?

Caiaphas. Thirty pieces of silver, and they shall at once be counted out to thee.

Dathan. Hearken, Judas, thirty pieces of silver ! What a gain !

Nathanael. And observe also, Judas, that is not all. If thou carriest out thy work well thou wilt be further cared for.

Priest. Thou mayest yet become a rich and illustrious man.

Judas. I am content. (*Aside*) Now is my fortune made !

Caiaphas. Rabbi, bring the thirty pieces of silver out of the treasury, and reckon them in the presence of the Council. Is this as ye will ?

Priests. Yea, it is so.

Nicodemus. How can ye conclude such a godless bargain ? (*To* JUDAS) And thou, vile creature, thou blushest not to sell thy Lord and Master, O forgetful of God—traitor, whom the earth shall swallow up ! Is thy most loving Friend and Benefactor to be sold by thee for thirty pieces of silver ?

Priests. Trouble not thyself, Judas, about the speech of this zealot. Let him be a disciple of the false Prophet ; thou dost thy duty as a disciple of Moses whilst thou servest the rightful authorities.

Rabbi (*enters with the money*). Come, Judas, take the thirty pieces of silver, and be a man ! (*He reckons them to him on a small stone table, so that they fall with a sharp sound* ; JUDAS *sweeps them eagerly into his bag.*)

Judas. Ye may depend upon my word.

Priests. But, besides, thou must carry out the work before the Feast.

Judas. Even now the fairest opportunity presents itself. Even in this night He will be in your hands. Give me armed men, that He may be duly surrounded.

Annas. Let us go forthwith, with the watch of the Temple.

Priests. Yea, yea, let us order them off.

Caiaphas. It would also be advisable to send some members of the holy Sanhedrim.

Priests. We are ready.   [CAIAPHAS *chooses out four deputies.*

Caiaphas. But, Judas, how will the band know the Master in the darkness of the night ?

Judas. They must come with torches and lanterns, and I will give them a sign.

Priests. Excellent, Judas!

Judas. Now I will hasten away to spy out everything. Then I will return to fetch the armed men.

Dathan. I will go with thee, Judas, and not leave thy side till thy work is accomplished.

Judas. At the gate of Bethphage I await your men.

[*Exit* JUDAS, DATHAN, *and the four deputies.*

SCENE III.

The Sanhedrim.

Caiaphas. All goes on admirably, venerable Fathers. But now our business is to look the great question in the face. What is to happen to this Man when God shall have given Him into our hands?

Priests. Let Him be buried alive in the deepest dungeon.

Caiaphas. Which of you will warrant that, in the tumult of an insurrection raised by them, His friends do not set Him free, or bribe the guards? Or might He not, through His wicked magic, break His bonds? (*The Priests are silent.*) I see well that ye know of no resource. Listen, then, to the High Priest. It is better that one man die, and that the whole nation perish not. He must DIE! Until He be dead there is no peace for Israel! No security for the law of Moses, no quiet hours for us.

Rabbi. God has spoken through his High Priest! through His death alone the people of Israel can and must be saved!

Nathanael. The word has long been upon my lips. Now is it spoken. Let Him die, the foe of our fathers!

Priests (*one to another*). Yea, let Him die! In His death is our salvation.

Annas. By my grey hairs I swear I will not rest until our shame be effaced in the blood of this Seducer!

Nicodemus. So judgment is pronounced upon this Man before He Himself be heard, before any trial, or any hearing of witnesses has taken place? Is this a transaction worthy of the fathers of the people of Israel?

Priests. What need is there here of inquiry or of witnesses? Have we not ourselves been witnesses of His words and deeds against the law?

Nicodemus. Ye are in yourselves accusers, witnesses, and judges. I have listened to His lofty teaching, I have seen His mighty works. They call for faith and for admiration, not for contempt and punishment.

Caiaphas. What, the wicked wretch deserves admiration! Thou wilt cleave to Moses, and yet defend that which condemns Moses?

Priests. Away with thee out of our assembly!

Joseph of Arimathea. I must agree with Nicodemus. No action has been imputed to Jesus of Nazareth which makes Him guilty of death. He has done nothing, save good.

Caiaphas. Speakest thou also thus? Is it not everywhere known how He has violated the sabbath, and how He has seduced the people with seditious words? Hath He not, as a Deceiver, wrought His pretended miracles through Beelzebub? Hath He not given Himself out as God?

Priests. Dost thou hear?

Joseph of Arimathea. Envy and malice have distorted His words and imputed evil motives to His noblest actions. And that He is God His divine works make manifest.

Nathanael. Ha, thou art known! For a long time already thou hast been a secret adherent of this Galilæan. Now hast thou fully revealed thyself.

Annas. So we have even in our midst a traitor to the holy laws, and even hitherto hath a seducer cast his nets?

Caiaphas. What doest thou here, thou rebel? Go after thy Prophet to see Him once more before His hour strike, for He must die! That is unalterably resolved.

Priests. Yea, He must die, that is our resolve!

Nicodemus. I execrate this resolution. I will have no part in this shameful and bloody judgment.

Joseph of Arimathea. I also will shun the spot where innocence is murdered.   [*Exeunt* NICODEMUS *and* JOSEPH.

SCENE IV.

The Sanhedrim.

Priest. At length we are quit of those traitors; we can now speak out freely.

Caiaphas. It will above all be necessary that we should sit formally in judgment upon this Man, hear Him, and bring witnesses against Him; otherwise the people will believe that we have only prosecuted Him out of envy and hatred.

Priest. Witnesses will not be wanting, I will provide them.

Pharisee. Our sentence stands. But in order that the weak do not take offence we will observe the forms of justice.

Second Pharisee. If these forms be not sufficient then will the strength of our will supply the want.

Rabbi. A little more or less guilty is of small importance. The public welfare requires His immediate death.

Caiaphas. As to what further belongs to the execution of the judgment, it would be best if we could obtain our end through the Governor, so that *he* should condemn Him to death. Then we should be without responsibility.

Nathanael. We can attempt it. If it does not succeed it still remains open to us to cause our judgment to be carried out by our trusty agents in the tumult of an insurrection of the people, without openly taking part in it ourselves.

Rabbi. And in the last resort a hand will easily be found which in the stillness of the dungeon will deliver the holy Sanhedrim from its enemy.

Caiaphas. Circumstances will teach us what must be done. For the present let us break up. But hold yourselves ready at every hour of the night. I may have you called. There is no time to lose. Our resolve is, He must die!

All (tumultuously). Let Him die, the enemy of our holy law!

ACT VII.

JESUS IN THE GARDEN OF GETHSEMANE.

PROLOGUE.

As Adam strives with bitter heart-weariness, exhausted in strength, in the sweat of his face, in order, alas! to expiate his own guilt, so does the guilt of mankind press upon the Redeemer. Overwhelmed by an ocean of sadness, His head bowed to earth with a heavy burden, running down with the bloody sweat of anguish, He wages the hottest fight in the olive-garden. Already the faithless Disciple, Iscariot, draws near, as leader of the Band of Men, using shamefully the seal of love as the token of betrayal. Thus basely, also, Joab dealt with Amasa; he presses at the same time, with hypocritical mien, the kiss of friendship upon his lips, and in his heart, alas! the dagger's point.

Chorus.

Judas, ach! verschlang den Bissen	Judas, lo, ate hallowed Bread
Bei dem Abendmahle	At the Sacrament,
Mit unheiligem Gewissen—	With unhallowed conscience—
Und der Satan fuhr sogleich in ihn.—	Satan quickly to him enter'd.—
Was du thun willst, sprach der Herr,	"That thou doest," spake the Master
Judas!—dieses thu' geschwind.—	"Judas!—see thou do it quickly."

F

Und er
Eilte aus dem Speisesaale
In die Synagoge hin
    Und verkaufte seinen Meister.

From the guest-room went he out,
Hastened to the Synagogue,
    And his Master there he sold.

Bald ist vollbracht—bald ist vollbracht
    Die schrecklichste der Thaten,
Ach ! heute noch, in dieser Nacht
    Wird Judas Ihn verrathen,
O kommet Alle,—kommet dann,
Und sehet mit die Leiden an.

Soon completed—soon is ended
    The most horrible of deeds.
Alas ! to-day, e'en in this night,
    Judas his Master will betray.
O come ye all—come then, O come—
Behold with us the Sufferings.

Im Schatten erst—und bald im Lichte
    Erscheinet sie—
Die traurigste Geschichte
    Von Gethsemani.

In shadow first—and soon in light
    Appeareth now
The mournfullest of histories,
    Gethsemane !

FIRST TABLEAU.—ADAM AND EVE LABOURING.

O wie sauer, o wie heiss,
    Wird es Vater Adam nicht !
Ach ! es fällt ein Strom von Schweiss
    Ueber Stirn und Angesicht.
Dieses ist die Frucht der Sünde,
    Gottes Fluch drückt die Natur ;
Darum gibt bei saurem Schweisse
Und bei mühevollem Fleisse
    Sie die Früchte sparsam nur.

O what labour, O what heat
    Must not Father Adam bear !
Ah ! a stream of sweat runs down
    Over brow and countenance.
This is the fruit of sin.
    God's curse oppresseth Nature,
Therefore yields she for hard sweat
And for toilsome industry
    Only sparingly her fruits.

So wird's unserm Jesus heiss,
    Wenn Er auf dem Oelberg ringt,
Dass ein Strom von blut'gem Schweiss
    Ihm durch alle Glieder dringt.
Dieses ist der Kampf der Sünde,
    Für uns Kämpfet ihn der Herr,
Kämpfet ihn in seinem Blute,
Zittert, bebet; doch mit Muthe
    Trinkt den Kelch der Leiden er.

Thus so sharp it is to Jesu
    (When 'mid olive shades He strives)
That a stream of bloody sweat
    From each holy limb is forced.
This is the strife of sin ;
    In His own Blood combats He—
Trembles—reels—yet with high heart
Drinks the cup of suffering.

SECOND TABLEAU.—THE MURDER OF AMASA BY JOAB.

Chorus.

Den Auftritt bei den Felsen Gabaon—
Den wiederholet Judas—Simon's Sohn.
    Ihr Felsen Gabaon !
Warum steht ihr ohne Zierde—
Sonst des Landes stolze Würde—
Wie mit einem Trauerflor umhüllet da ?

The scene near Gibeon's rocks—
Judas repeateth—Simon's son.
    Ye rocks of Gibeon !
Why stand ye thus unhonoured—
Ye, late the land's proud boast—
As though with mourning veil wrapt round ?

Saget, ich beschwör' euch, saget : Was
    geschah?

                    Was geschah ?

Say, I adjure thee, say—what deed was
    done ?

                    What deed was done ?

Flieht, Wanderer! flieht schnell von hier;
Verflucht sei dieser blutgedüngte Ort!
Da fiel von einer Meuchlershand durch-
bohrt
　　　　Ein Amasa,
Vertrauend auf der heil'gen Freundschaft
Gruss
Getäuscht durch Joabs falschen Bruder-
kuss.

O ruft in uns're Stimme:—Der Fluch sei
dir!
Die Felsen klagen über dich;
Die blutgedüngte Erde rächet sich.—
Verstummet, Felsen Gabaon mit eurer
Stimme,
Und hört und spaltet euch vor Grimme.
　Ihr Felsen Gabaon!
　So verräth den Menschensohn.
　Ach! mit heuchlerischem Grusse
　Und mit einem falschen Kusse
　　Als der Führer einer Rott'
　Judas, der Iskariot.
　Ihr Felsen Gabaon:
Vernehmet unsern Schwur,
Und fluchet diesem Scheusal der
Natur!

Ihm flucht das ganze Erdenrund,
Eröffne, Erde, deinen Schlund!—
Verschlinge ihn!—der Hölle Feu'r
Verzehre dieses Ungeheu'r!

Fly, wanderer, with speed fly hence!
Accursed be this blood-stained spot!
Pierced by assassin's hand here fell
　　　　One Amasa,
In holy friendship's greeting trusting,
By Joab's false brother-kiss deceived.

With one voice cry with us:—Curse on
thee!
The rocks complain of thee,
The blood-soaked earth takes vengeance.
Be silent, rocks of Gibeon!—Silent your
voice,
And hear, and split yourselves with rage,
　Ye rocks of Gibeon!
　So betrays the Son of man,
　Ah, with hypocrite's vile greeting,
　And with false deceiving kiss,
　　As the leader of a band,
　Judas, the Iscariot.
　Ye rocks of Gibeon!
Receive our oath,
And this monster of all Nature curse!

All Earth's circle curseth him,
Open thine abyss, O Earth!
Swallow him!—and let hell-fire
Consume this monster dire!

SCENE I.

A Road near the Mount of Olives.—JUDAS *and the Four Deputies of the Sanhedrim.*—The TRADERS.—SELPHA, *the Leader of the Band.*— MALCHUS.—*A Band of Men.*

Judas. Now, be watchful. We are nearing the place whither the Master has withdrawn Himself in order to pass the still night in this lonely region. Resistance need not be thought of, the surprise is too unexpected.

Soldier. Should they venture it, they will feel the strength of our arms.

Judas. Do not fear it. He will fall into your hands without a sword's stroke.

Traders. But how shall we know the Master in the darkness?

Judas. I will give you this as a sign. When we are in the garden— give heed—I will hasten to Him. Whomsoever I shall kiss that same is He. Hold Him fast.

Priest. Good. This sign makes us go on more securely. Do ye hear ? By the kiss ye shall know the Master.

Soldiers. We will give heed enough.

Judas. Now let us hasten. It is time. We are now not far from the garden.

Pharisee. Judas, if to-night brings us this happy chance thy action will bring thee forth most excellent fruit.

Traders. From us also thou shalt receive a handsome recompense.

Soldiers. Come, now, Thou stirrer up of the people! Now shalt Thou receive Thy reward.   [*Exeunt omnes.*

SCENE II. (See p. 16.)

The Garden of Olives.— CHRIST *and the* DISCIPLES *advance together out of the Background.*

Christ. Verily, verily, I say unto you, Ye shall weep and lament, but the world shall rejoice ; ye shall be sorrowful, but your sorrow shall be turned into joy. For I will see you again, and your heart shall rejoice, and your joy no man taketh from you. I came forth from the Father, and am come into the world : again I leave the world and go to the Father.

Peter. Lo, now speakest Thou plainly, and speakest no proverb.

James the Great. Now are we sure that Thou knowest all things.

Thomas. By this we believe that Thou camest forth from God.

Christ. Do ye now believe ? Behold, the hour cometh, yea, is now come, that ye shall be scattered every man to his own, and shall leave me alone : and yet I am not alone, for the Father is with me. Yea, Father, the hour is come ! Glorify Thy Son, that Thy Son also may glorify Thee. I have finished the work which Thou gavest me to do ; I have manifested Thy name unto the men which Thou gavest me out of the world. Holy Father, keep them through Thine own name. Sanctify them in the truth. Neither pray I for these alone, but for them also which shall believe on me through their word ; that they all may be one, as Thou, Father, art in me, and I in Thee. Father, I will that they also whom Thou hast given me be with me where I am ; that they may behold my glory which Thou hast given me ; for Thou lovedst me before the foundation of the world. (*To the* DISCIPLES, *entering the garden in visible sadness*) Children, sit ye here while I go and pray yonder. Pray that ye enter not into temptation. But ye, Peter, James, and John, follow me.
                    [*He goes forward with the three* APOSTLES.

Disciples (*in the background*). What has happened to our Master ? We never yet saw Him so sorrowful. Not in vain has the Master prepared us for it beforehand.

Christ (*in the foreground*). O beloved children ! my soul is exceeding sorrowful, even unto death : tarry ye here and watch with me.

(*After a pause*) I will go a little further, in order to strengthen myself by communion with my Father.

[*He goes to a rocky place with slow and tottering steps.*

Peter (*gazes after Him*). O most good and dear Master!

John. My soul suffers with the soul of our Teacher. (*They sit down.*)

Peter. I am full of fear! We were witnesses of His transfiguration on the mount. But now—what must we see?

Christ (*near the rocky ground*). This hour must come upon me—the hour of darkness. But for this hour came I into the world. (*He falls upon His knees.*) Father! my Father! if it be possible—and all things are possible unto Thee—let this cup pass from me! (*He falls upon His face and remains so for awhile, then again kneels.*) Yet, Father, not as I will, but as Thou wilt! (*He stands up, looks up to heaven, then goes to the three* DISCIPLES.) Simon!

Peter (*as in a dream*). Alas, my Master!

Christ. Simon, sleepest thou?

Peter. Master, here am I!

Christ. Could ye not watch with me one hour?

Apostles. Rabbi, sleep has overmastered us.

Christ. Watch and pray, that ye enter not into temptation.

Apostles. Yea, Master, we will pray and watch.

Christ. The spirit indeed is willing, but the flesh is weak. (*He returns to the rocky ground.*) My Father, Thy demand is righteous, Thy counsels are holy, Thou claimest this sacrifice! (*He falls upon His knees.*) Father! the struggle is fierce. (*He falls upon His face, then raises Himself.*) Yet if this cup may not pass away from me except I drink it, my Father, Thy will be done. (*He stands up.*) Most Holy! in holiness shall it be accomplished by me! (*He returns to the sleeping* DISCIPLES.) Are then your eyes so heavy that ye could not watch? O my most trusted ones! even amongst you I find none to comfort me! (*He goes towards the rocky ground, then pauses.*) Ah! how dark all around me becomes! The sorrows of death take hold upon me! The burden of divine justice lies upon me! O sinners! O sins of mankind! ye weigh me down! O fearful burden! O the bitterness of this cup! (*He comes to the rocky ground.*) My Father! (*He kneels.*) If it be not possible that these sins pass away from me, Thy will be done! Thy most holy will! Father!—Thy Son!—Hear Him!

SCENE III.

An ANGEL appears.

Angel. Son of man, sanctify the Father's will! Consider the blessedness which shall proceed from Thy struggle! The Father has laid upon Thee, and Thou hast of Thy free will taken upon Thee, to become the offering for sinful humanity : carry it through ! The Father will glorify Thee.

Christ. Yea, most holy Father, I adore Thy providence, I will accomplish it—accomplish it ! To reconcile, to save, to bring blessedness ! (*He rises.*) Strengthened through Thy word, O Father, I go joyfully to meet that to which Thou hast called me, the substitute for sinful man ! (*To the three* DISCIPLES) Sleep on now and take your rest.

Peter. What is it, Master ?

The three Apostles. Behold, we are ready !

Christ. The hour is come. The Son of man is betrayed into the hands of sinners. Rise, let us be going.

Disciples. What tumult is that ?

Philip. Come, let us gather around the Master.

[*The* DISCIPLES *hasten forwards.*

Christ. Lo, he that betrayeth me is at hand.

[JUDAS *appears with the Band.*

Andrew. What does this multitude want ?

All. Ah, all is over with us !

John. And see, Judas is at their head !

SCENE IV.

Judas. Hail, Master ! (*He kisses* JESUS.)

Christ. Friend, wherefore art thou come ? Betrayest thou the Son of man with a kiss ? (*He goes towards the Band of Men.*) Whom seek ye ?

Soldiers. Jesus of Nazareth.

Christ. I am He.

Soldiers. Woe unto us ! What is this ? (*They fall to the ground.*)

Disciples. A single word from Him casts them to the ground !

Christ (*to the men*). Fear not, arise !

Disciples. Lord, cast them down that they rise not up again.

Christ. Whom seek ye ?

Band of Men. Jesus of Nazareth.

Christ. I have told you that I am He. If, therefore, ye seek me, let these go their way.

Selpha. Seize Him ! (*The servants approach* JESUS.)

Peter and Philip. Lord, shall we smite with the sword ?

[PETER *strikes* MALCHUS.

Malchus. Alas ! I am wounded, mine ear is cut off !

Christ (*to the* DISCIPLES). Suffer ye thus far. (*To* MALCHUS) Be not troubled, thou shalt be healed. (*He touches* MALCHUS' *ear. Then to* PETER) Put up thy sword into the sheath, for all they that take the sword shall perish with the sword. The cup which my Father hath given me, shall I not drink it ? Thinkest thou that I cannot now pray to my

Father and He shall presently give me more than twelve legions of angels? But how then shall the Scriptures be fulfilled, that thus it must be? (*To the* PHARISEES) Are ye come out as against a thief with swords and staves for to take me? I sat daily with you teaching in the Temple and ye stretched forth no hands against me, and took me not. But this is your hour and the power of darkness. Behold, I am here!

Selpha. Take Him, and bind Him fast, that He escape not.

Nathanael. You are responsible for it to the Sanhedrim.

[*The* DISCIPLES *forsake Him.*

Band of Men. Out of our hands He escapes not.

Traders. Now will we cool our revenge.

Nathanael. First go we to Annas, the High Priest. Lead Him thither.

Trader (to JUDAS). Judas, thou art a man! Thou knowest how to keep thy word.

Judas. Said I not to you that to-night He should be in your power?

Pharisee. Thou hast laid the whole Sanhedrim under obligation to thee.

Band of Men (driving JESUS *before them).* On with Thee! At Jerusalem they will decide about Thee.

Selpha. Let us hasten ; lead Him away safely.

Band of Men. Ha! run now, as Thou hast run about the land of Judæa.

Selpha. Spare Him not! Urge Him on.

Band of Men. Forward, otherwise Thou shalt be driven with sticks!

Traders. Doth Beelzebub then aid Thee no longer? [*Exeunt omnes.*

SCENE V.

PETER *and* JOHN *coming out of their Hiding-place.*

Peter. Alas, they have taken Him away, our good Master, John! (*Weeps upon his bosom.*) That which is incredible comes to pass.

John. O Friend, O best of Teachers! Is this then Thine end? Is this then the thanks for the goodness of which Thou hast been the author? The Benefactor of the people, the Friend of humanity, in chains!

Peter. John, I will go after our Master. I must see Him yet again. Whither have they dragged Him off?

John. Didst thou not hear?—to Annas. Come, we will go together.

[*Exeunt.*

END OF THE FIRST PART.

PART II.

From the Arrest in the Garden of Gethsemane to the Condemnation under Pilate.

ACT VIII.

JESUS *before* ANNAS. (*See* p. 17.)

PROLOGUE.

O fearful night! Behold the Redeemer! He is dragged from tribunal to tribunal, and everywhere encounters injury and ill-treatment. A wretch repays Him for a sincere word, spoken to Annas,—strikes Him with rough hand on His blessed face in order to gain praise for himself. Such shameful reward was also the reward of Micaiah, when he revealed the truth to King Ahab; one of the lying prophets struck him on the cheek. Truth earns only hate and persecution; yet, though its light may be avoided and banished, at last it will conquer, and break through the darkness!

Chorus.

Begonnen ist der Kampf der Schmerzen—	Pain's battle dread has now begun—
Begonnen ist Gethsemani.	Begun Gethsemane.
O Sünder! nehmet es zu Herzen	O sinners! lay it to your hearts,
Vergesset diese Scene nie!	And ne'er forget this scene!
Für euer Heil ist das geschehen,	For your salvation, that befell
Was auf dem Oelberg wir gesehen.	Which now we saw 'mid olive shades.
Für euch betrübt bis in den Tod	Sorrowful even unto death,
Sank er zur Erde nieder,	For you He sank upon the ground;
Für euch drang ihm, wie Blut so roth,	For you the sweat as blood was forced
Der Schweiss durch alle Glieder.	From every agonized limb.
Begonnen ist der Kampf, &c.	Pain's battle dread, &c.

TABLEAU.—THE PROPHET MICAIAH BEFORE KING AHAB SMITTEN ON THE CHEEK.

Chorus.

Wer frei die Wahrheit spricht,	Who boldly speaks the truth
Den schlägt man in's Gesicht.	Is smitten in the face.
Michäas, er wagte es die Wahrheit laut zu sagen	Micaiah dared to speak the truth,
Und ward in's Angesicht geschlagen.	And on the cheek was struck.

" König, du wirst unterliegen,
Solltest Ramoth du bekriegen : "
　　Diess ist, was Michäas spricht.
" Dich von Unglück dann zu retten,
Glaube, König, Baals Propheten—
　　Dieser Schmeichler Lügen nicht ! "

Doch die Wahrheit des Michäas
　　Schmeichelt einem Achab nicht ;
Und der Lügner Sedekias
　　Schlägt dafür ihn in's Gesicht.

Lügner, Heuchler, Schmeichler pflücken
　　Rosen, Lorbeer ohne Müh' !
Nur die Wahrheit muss sich bücken,
　　Denn die Wahrheit schmeichelt nie.

Jesum über seine Lehren,
Seine Thaten zu verhören,
　　Räumt das Recht sich Annas ein.
" Um zu wissen, was ich lehrte,
Frage Jeden, der mich hörte,"
　　Wird die Rede Jesu sein.

Doch die Wahrheit auf die Fragen
　　Schmeichelt einem Annas nicht ;
Und die Unschuld wird geschlagen—
　　Jesus in das Angesicht.

" O King, thou wilt be conquered
Should Ramoth fight with thee : "
　　These words Micaiah spoke.
" Then to save thyself from mishap,
Of Baal's prophets trust not, King,
　　Falsehoods—flattering though they be."

But Micaiah's truthful message
　　Flatters not King Ahab's soul ;
And the liar, Zedekiah,
　　Strikes him for it in the face.

Liars, flatt'rers, hypocrites,
　　Roses, laurels pluck with ease !
Truth alone must needs stoop low,
　　For truth never flatters men.

Jesus (touching His high teaching
And His works) to hear, the right
　　Annas to himself assumes.
" Wouldst thou know what I have taught,
Ask of those who heard my words."
　　This will Jesu's answer be.

But the truthful words he hears
　　Flatter not the soul of Annas ;
Innocence receives a blow—
　　Jesus in the face is smitten.

SCENE I.

The High Priest ANNAS *with three* PRIESTS *on the Balcony of his House.*

Annas. I can find no rest this night until I know that this agitator is in our hands. Full of longing I await my trusty servants with the news that the enemy of the Sanhedrim is already in fetters.

Priests. They cannot long delay ; it is a long time since they broke up.

Annas. In vain has my troubled gaze been fixed over and over upon the street of Kedron. (*The* PRIESTS *try to tranquillize* ANNAS, *and two of them go out in different directions to see if the Band of Men be near ; one hastens towards the Kedron-gate, and one towards the Siloa-gate. At last one Priest returns and announces that all has gone well.*)

Annas. Auspicious message, happy hour ! A stone is taken from off my heart, and I feel as though new-born. Now, for the first time, I call myself with joy High Priest of the chosen people !

SCENE II.

The Four Deputies of the Sanhedrim appear with JUDAS *upon the Balcony.*

The four Pharisees. Long live our High Priest !

Nathanael. The wish of the Sanhedrim is fulfilled !

Annas. O, I must embrace you for joy !   Judas, thy name will take an honourable place in our records of the year.   Even before the feast shall the Galilæan die !

Judas (terrified). Die?

Annas. His death is resolved upon.

Judas. I will not be responsible for His life and for His blood.

Annas. That is not necessary, He is in our power.

Judas. I did not deliver Him to you for that end.

Pharisee. Thou hast delivered Him, the rest is our business.

Judas. Woe is me !   What have I done?   Shall He die?   No! I did not desire that.   I will not have it !   [*He hastens away.*

Pharisees (jeering at him). Thou mayest wish it or not, but He must die.

SCENE III.

The same without JUDAS.   *Directly after, enter upon the Balcony* CHRIST, SELPHA, *the Leader of the Band and the Temple, Servants,* MALCHUS, *and* BALBUS.   *The Band remains underneath.*

Priest. High Priest, the Prisoner is on the threshold.

Annas. Let Him be brought before me.

                          [SELPHA *appears with* CHRIST.

Annas. Have ye brought Him alone Prisoner?

Balbus. His followers dispersed themselves like frightened sheep.

Selpha. We found it not worth the trouble of apprehending them. Nevertheless Malchus nearly lost his life.

Annas. What happened?

Selpha. One of His followers, with a drawn sword, smote him, and cut off his ear.

Annas. How?   But there is no mark of it.

Balbus (mocking). The magician has conjured it back upon him again.

Annas. What sayest thou about it, Malchus?

Malchus (gravely). I cannot explain it.   A wonderful thing has happened to me.

Annas. Has the Deceiver perchance also bewitched thee?   (*To* JESUS) Tell me, by what power hast Thou done this?   [CHRIST *is silent.*

Selpha. Speak, when Thy High Priest questions Thee !

Annas. Speak! Give an account of Thy disciples, and of Thy teaching, which Thou hast spread abroad in the whole of Judæa, and with which Thou hast seduced the people.

Christ. I spake openly to the world; I ever taught in the Synagogue and in the Temple, and in secret have I said nothing. Why askest thou me? Ask them which heard me, what I have said unto them: behold, they know what I said.

Balbus (*strikes* JESUS). Answerest Thou the High Priest so?

Christ. If I have spoken evil, bear witness of the evil; but if well, why smitest thou me?

Annas. Wilt Thou still defy us, when Thy life and death are in our power? I am weary of this wicked wretch!

Balbus (*to* CHRIST, *who is led away*). Wait awhile, Thy obstinacy will give way.

Annas. I will betake myself for a while to repose, or rather to quiet reflection as to how that which is happily begun may be brought to an end. In any case I shall receive the summons to the Sanhedrim early in the morning. 　　　　　　　　　　　　　　　　　　　[*Exeunt omnes.*

SCENE IV.

CHRIST *in the midst of the Band of Men.*

Men (*to* SELPHA, *who leads* JESUS). Ha! is His business already over?

Selpha. His defence went badly.

Balbus. It was, however, worth a good blow on the face to Him.

Selpha. Take Him now, and away with Him to the palace of Caiaphas.

Band of Men. Away with Him! March!

Balbus. Be joyful! from Caiaphas Thou wilt have a still better reception.

Band of Men. There will the ravens already sing about Thy ears!

SCENE V.

PETER *and* JOHN *before the House of* ANNAS.—*A* PRIEST.

Peter. How will it go here with the dearest Master? O John, how sorrowful I am concerning Him!

John. Surely He will have had to suffer scorn and ill-treatment here. I am very anxious to get near the house.

Peter. All around, however, is so quiet.

John. No noise is heard in the palace. Will they have led Him away again?

Priest (coming out). What do ye want here at the palace in the night-time?

John. Pardon, we saw from afar a crowd of people going here through the Kedron-gate, and we went after them to see what had happened.

Priest. They brought a Prisoner, but He has already been sent to Caiaphas.

John. To Caiaphas? Then we will go away at once.

Priest. It will be as well for you, otherwise I would have you taken up as night brawlers.

Peter. We will raise no commotion and go away quietly.   [*Exeunt.*

Priest (looking after them). Are they perchance followers of the Galilæan? If I only knew! However, they will not escape our people if they go to Caiaphas' palace. The whole following must be destroyed, otherwise the people will never be brought into subjection.   [*Exit.*

ACT IX.

JESUS BEFORE CAIAPHAS. (*See* pp. 17–19.)

PROLOGUE.

Before enraged enemies, now His judges, stands the Lord, veiled in silence. Patiently He hears all the accusations and lies, even the sentence of death. As once Naboth, though innocent, was persecuted, and condemned through false witness as a blasphemer of God, so also He whose only fault is—Truth, Love, Beneficence. Soon shall ye see Him surrounded by inhuman servants, given up as a mark to the brutality of scorn, spitefully entreated amidst wild laughter. In patient Job, laden with reproach even by his friends in his deepest trouble, ye see foreshadowed the heavenly meekness of the beloved Saviour.

Chorus.

Wie blutet mir das Herz!	How sore my heart doth bleed!
Der Heiligste steht vor Gericht.	'Fore judgment stands the Holiest.
Muss er der Sünder Bosheit tragen;	The crimes of sinners He must bear;
Verrathen und beschimpft—gebunden und geschlagen:	Betray'd and scorn'd, smitten and bound.
Wem zittert nicht im Auge eine Thräne?—	Whose eyes will not be full of tears?—
Von Annas weg zu Kaiphas fortgerissen—	From Annas, dragg'd to Caiaphas—
Was wird er da, ach! leiden müssen!	What must He suffer there, alas!
Seht hier im Bilde diese neue Leidensscene.	See here in type this suff'ring fresh.

FIRST TABLEAU.—THE DEATH OF NABOTH.

" Es sterbe Naboth ! fort mit ihm zum Tod !
Gelästert, König ! dich, gelästert hat er
    Gott :
    Er sei vertilgt aus Israel ! "
So geifern wild die Lästerzungen —
    Von einer losen Jezabel
Zu einem falschen Eid gedungen.

Ach ! mit dem Tode rächet man,
    Was Naboth nie verbrochen ;—
Der Weinberg wird dem König dann
    Von Schurken zugesprochen.

Diess ist ein treues Bild der Welt,
    So geht's noch öfters heute.
Das arme fromme Lämmchen fällt
    Dem starken Wolf zur Beute.

Ihr mächt'gen Götter dieser Welt—
Zum Wohl der Menschheit aufgestellt—
Vergesst bei Uebung eurer Pflicht
Des unsichtbaren Richters nicht !
Bei ihm sind alle Menschen gleich,
Sie mögen dürftig oder reich,
    Geadelt oder Bettler Sein ;—
    Gerechtigkeit gilt ihm allein.

" Let Naboth die ! To death with him !
He hath blasphemed thee, O King !

    And God!—from Israel cast him out !"
Thus foaming cry the sland'rous tongues,
    By Jezebel, the wicked Queen,
Paid for their false and evil oath.

Alas ! with death they vengeance take
    On that which Naboth ne'er had done ;
The vineyard then upon the King
    By wicked rogues is then bestow'd.

Of this world 'tis an image true,
    So goes it often e'en to-day.
The poor and gentle lamb doth fall
    To the strong wolf an easy prey.

Ye mighty gods of this poor earth—
For weal of men above them placed—
Forget not, 'mid your duties' round,
The invisible Judge of all.
Before Him all the sons of men
Are equal, be they poor or rich,
    Noble or born of beggar race ;
    He cares for righteousness alone.

SECOND TABLEAU.—THE AFFLICTION OF JOB.

Seht ! welch ein Mensch ! Ach ! ein
    Gerippe
Ein Graus—ein Ekel der Natur.
Wie windet sich um Wang und Lippe
Ein ausgedörrtes Häutchen nur.

Seht ! welch ein Mensch ! Ach ! wie
    geschunden
Sieht man bis auf das Mark hinein.
Das Eiter träuft aus seinen Wunden.
Und Fäulung frisst schon sein Gebein.

Ach ! welch ein Mensch ! Ein Job in
    Schmerzen
Ach ! wem entlockt er Thränen nicht !
Sein Weib doch—seine Freunde scherzen
Und spotten seiner in's Gesicht.

Ach ! welch ein Mensch !
Wer mag ihn einen Menschen nennen ?
Vom Fusse hin bis an sein Haupt
Wird aller Zierde er beraubt.

Behold the man ! a skeleton,

A fright—of nature loathsomeness !—
To cheek and lips how fearfully
Only the withered skin adheres !

Behold the man ! the putrid wounds

No whole part in his body leave.
Corruption flows from every sore,
And rottenness devours his bones.

Behold the man ! A Job in pain,

Ah, whom doth he not move to tears ?
His friends and e'en his wife make sport,
Before him mocking at his woe.

    Behold the man !
Yet who may call him still a man ?
From head to foot his body now
Despoiled of every grace is seen.

Ach ! welch ein Mensch !	Behold the man !
Ihr Augen ! weinet heisse Thränen.	O eyes ! weep warmest tears of grief.
Ach ! Jesus—ach ! ein Mensch nicht mehr !	Ah Jesu—*Thou* a man no more !
Der Menschen Spott und Hohn wird er.	The scorn and jest of men is He.
Ach ! welch ein Mensch !	Behold the man !
O alle ihr gerührten Herzen !	O all ye moved and grieved hearts !
Ach ! Jesus, Jesus ! Gottes Sohn	Ah Jesu, Jesu, Son of God,
Wird loser Knechte Spott und Hohn	Becomes the scorn and jest of knaves
Bei endelosem Kampf der Schmerzen.	Amid His endless strife of pain.
Ach ! welch ein Mensch !	Behold the man !

SCENE I.

Band of Men.—CHRIST *led through the Streets.*

Band of Men (making a noise). Thou wilt become a spectacle—a spectacle to the whole nation !

Balbus. Hurry Thyself ! Thy followers are quite ready. They wish to proclaim Thee King of Israel.

Band of Men. Thou hast often dreamed of it, hast Thou not ?

Selpha. Caiaphas the High Priest will now interpret this dream for Him.

Balbus. Hearest Thou ? Caiaphas will announce to Thee Thy exaltation.

Band of Men (with laughter). Yes, Thine exaltation between heaven and earth !

Selpha. Look out, ye fellows ! There, through Pilate's tower, lies our nearest way to the castle of Caiaphas. Station yourselves there in the outer court until further action.

Band of Men. Thy orders shall be carried out.   [*Exeunt.*

SCENE II.

CAIAPHAS *in his Sleeping-chamber.*—*The* PRIESTS *and* PHARISEES.

Caiaphas. The happy beginning promises us speedy accomplishment of our wishes. I thank you, noble members of the Sanhedrim, for your zealous and prudent co-operation !

Priest. The highest thanks are due to our High Priest.

Caiaphas. Let us now pursue our path without delay ! All is prepared beforehand. The Council will be immediately assembled, the necessary witnesses have been brought. I will now at once begin the trial of the Prisoner. Then judgment will be given and care taken for its execution. Trust me, my friends ! I have conceived a plan for myself and hope to carry it out.

All. The God of our fathers bless every action of our High Priest !

SCENE III.

The same.—The Band of Men bring in CHRIST.—*The False Witnesses.*

Selpha (the leader of the Band). Venerable High Priests, here is the Prisoner !

Caiaphas. Bring Him nearer, that I may look Him in the face.

Selpha. Stand forth, and show respect here to the House of the Sanhedrim.

Caiaphas. Thou art then He who hadst the fancy to wish to bring about the downfall of our synagogue and of the law of Moses? Thou art accused of stirring up the people to disobedience, of despising the holy traditions of the fathers, of many times transgressing the Divine command of keeping the Sabbath holy, and of many blasphemous words and deeds against God. There are here worthy men, who are ready to uphold the truth of these complaints with their witness. Listen to them, and then Thou mayest defend Thyself if Thou canst.

First Witness. I can testify before God that this Man has stirred up the people, while He has openly denounced the members of the Council and the Scribes as hypocrites, raging wolves in sheeps' clothing, blind leaders of the blind, and has said that no one is to follow them.

Second Witness. I also witness to this, and can add besides that He has forbidden the people to pay tribute to Cæsar.

First Witness. Yea, at least He has let fall ambiguous words concerning it.

Caiaphas. What sayest Thou to that? Thou art silent?

Third Witness. I have often seen how He with His disciples has, in defiance of the law, gone to table with unwashen hands, how He was wont to have friendly intercourse with publicans and sinners, and went into their houses to eat with them. (*Other Witnesses.* This we also have often seen.) I have heard from trustworthy people that He even spake with Samaritans, and indeed dwelt with them a whole day.

First Witness. I was also an eye-witness of how He did on the Sabbath what by God's law is forbidden, and fearlessly healed the sick. He has enticed others to break the Sabbath. And He has also commanded a man to carry his bed to his house.

Caiaphas. What hast Thou to reply to this evidence? Hast Thou nothing to answer to it?

Third Witness. Thou hast (I was present) taken upon Thyself to forgive sins, which belongs only to God. Thou hast also blasphemed God!

First Witness. Thou hast called God Thy Father, and hast dared to declare that Thou art One with the Father. Thou hast also made Thyself equal to God.

Second Witness. Thou hast exalted Thyself above our forefather Abraham ; Thou didst say that before Abraham was Thou already art.

Fourth Witness. Thou hast said, "I am able to destroy the Temple of God and to build it in three days."

Fifth Witness. I have heard Thee say, "I will destroy this Temple that is made with hands, and within three days I will build another, made without hands."

Caiaphas. Thou hast then extolled Thyself as a superhuman Divine authority! These are heavy accusations, and they are witnessed according to the law. Answer, if Thou canst! Thou thinkest to be able to save Thyself through silence. Thou darest not to acknowledge before the fathers of the people that which Thou hast taught before the people. Or darest Thou? Hear then: I, the High Priest, adjure Thee by the living God! say, art Thou the Messiah, the Son of the most High God?

Christ. Thou hast said it, I am. Nevertheless I say unto you, hereafter ye shall see the Son of man sitting on the right hand of power, and coming in the clouds of heaven.

Caiaphas. He hath blasphemed God! What need we any further witnesses? Ye have heard the blasphemy! What think ye?

All. He is guilty of death!

Caiaphas. He has been unanimously declared guilty of death. Yet not I, and not the Sanhedrim, but the law of God itself declares the judgment of death upon Him. Ye teachers of the law, I require you to reply, what saith the holy law of him who is disobedient to the authority ordained of God?

First Priest (reads). "The man that will do presumptuously, and will not hearken unto the priest that standeth to minister there before the Lord thy God, or unto the judge, even that man shall die: and thou shalt put away the evil from Israel."*

Caiaphas. What doth the law ordain concerning him who profaneth the Sabbath?

Second Priest (reads). "Ye shall keep the Sabbath therefore, for it is holy unto you: every one that defileth it shall surely be put to death: for whosoever doeth any work therein, that soul shall be cut off from his people."†

Caiaphas. How doth the law punish a blasphemer?

Third Priest (reads). "Speak unto the children of Israel, saying, Whosoever curseth his God shall bear his sin. And he that blasphemeth the name of the Lord he shall surely be put to death; all the congregation shall certainly stone him, as well the stranger as he that is born in the land."‡

Caiaphas. Thus is judgment declared upon this Jesus of Nazareth, declared according to the law, and it shall be carried out as soon as possible. Meanwhile I will have the Condemned safely kept. Lead Him away! Guard Him, and with the morning dawn bring Him to the great Sanhedrim.

* Deut. xvii, 12.   † Ex. xxxi. 14.   ‡ Lev. xxiv. 15, 16.

Selpha. Come on then, Messiah! We will show Thee Thy palace.
Balbus. There Thou wilt receive due homage. [*They lead Him away.*

SCENE IV.

Caiaphas. We are near our end! Now, however, determined steps are necessary!

All. We will not rest till He be brought to death.

Caiaphas. With the break of day let us re-assemble. Then shall the judgment be confirmed by the whole assembled Council, and the Prisoner shall be hereupon immediately brought before Pilate in order that he may enforce it, and so cause it to be carried out.

Priests. May God soon set us free from our Enemy! [*Exeunt omnes.*

SCENE V.

JUDAS *alone.*

Judas. Fearful forebodings drive me hither and thither. That word in the house of Annas—He must die! O! that word pursues me everywhere! No! they will not carry it so far! It were horrible—and I—the guilt of it! Here in the house of Caiaphas I will inquire how matters stand. Shall I go in? I can no longer bear them, these uncertainties, and I am terrified of attaining certainty, but it must come some time!

[*He goes in.*

SCENE VI.

Night.—Hall in the House of CAIAPHAS.*— The maids* SARAH *and* HAGAR, *with a Band of Men.—The Servants lie around a large brazier of coals.—*JOHN *and* PETER, *later* SELPHA, *with* CHRIST.

Hagar (*to* JOHN, *who stands at the entrance*). John, comest thou also hither in the middle of the night? Come in then. Here canst thou warm thyself. Will not ye, men, willingly make a little room for this young man?

Band of Men. Yea, truly, come in then!

John. Good Hagar, there is yet a companion with me; might he not also come in?

Hagar. Where is he? Let him come in. Wherefore should he stand without in the cold? (JOHN *goes to* PETER, *who is standing at one side, but returns alone.*) Now, where is he?

G

John. He is standing on the threshold, but dares not come in.

Hagar. Come in, good friend, be not afraid.

Band of Men. Friend, come thou also here to us.　Warm thyself.

[PETER *timidly approaches the fire.*

Servant. We still see and hear nothing of the Prisoner.

Band of Men. How much longer must we wait here?

Second Servant. Probably He will come from the audience as one condemned to death.

First Servant. I marvel if His disciples will not also be sought for.

Band of Men (*laughing*). That were a fine piece of work, if they were all to be taken prisoners.

Second Servant. It would not be worth while.　If the Master be once out of the way the Galilæans would take flight and no longer allow themselves to be seen in Jerusalem.

First Servant. But at least the one who in the garden took to his weapon and cut off Malchus' ear ought to receive sharp chastisement.

Band of Men. Yea, for it is said: "An ear for an ear!"

First Servant. Ha, ha, ha! but the rule does not apply here, for Malchus has got his ear back.

Hagar (*to* PETER). I have been observing thee for some time.　If I mistake not, thou art one of the disciples of the Galilæan?　Yea, yea, thou art.

Peter. I?　No—I am not.　Woman, I know Him not, neither know I what thou sayest.　　　[*He tries to slip away and passes near* SARAH.

Sarah. Behold, this fellow was also with Jesus of Nazareth!

Several. Art thou also one of His disciples?

Peter. I am not, on my soul!　I know not the Man. [*The cock crows.*

Third Servant. Behold this man! of a truth he also was with Him!

Peter. I know not what ye have to do with me.　What is this Man to me?

Several. Surely thou art one of them! for thou art a Galilæan, and thy speech bewrayeth thee.

Peter. May God be my witness that I know not this Man of whom ye speak!　　　[*The cock crows the second time.*

Fourth Servant. What, did I not see thee in the garden with Him when my cousin Malchus had his ear struck off?

Band of Men (*at the fire*). Make yourselves ready, they are bringing in the Prisoner!　　　[SELPHA *appears with* CHRIST.

Second Servant. Now, how have things gone?

Selpha. He is condemned to death.

Band of Men (*mocking*). Poor King!

[CHRIST *looks sorrowfully upon* PETER.

Selpha. Onwards, comrades! until the morning dawn we must watch Him.

Second Servant. Come, He will beguile the time for us.　　[*Exeunt.*

SCENE VII.

PETER *alone, afterwards* JOHN. (*See* p. 20.)

Peter. Ah, dearest Master, how deeply have I fallen! O weak, O wretched man! Thee, my most loving Friend and Teacher, I have denied—three times have I denied Thee for whom I promised to die. O, I know not how I could so terribly have forgotten myself! Accursed be my shameful betrayal! May my heart be ever filled with sorrow for this despicable cowardice! Lord, my dearest Lord, if Thou hast still grace left for me, grace for a faithless one, O grant it, grant it even to me! even now hearken to the voice of my repentant heart. Alas, the sin has been committed; I can never more undo it, but ever, ever will I weep and repent over it; never, never more will I leave Thee! O Thou most full of goodness, Thou wilt not cast me out? Thou wilt not despise my bitter repentance? No; the gentle compassionate glance with which Thou didst look on me, Thy deeply fallen disciple, assures me that Thou wilt forgive me. This hope I have in Thee, O best of Teachers. And the whole love of my heart shall from this moment belong to Thee, and keep me most closely united to Thee. Nothing, nothing shall be able ever again to separate me from Thee! [*Exit.*

John. Where can Peter be gone? Hath any mischance befallen him? Perchance I shall light upon him on the road. I will now go to Bethany. But, what will thy heart feel, most beloved Mother, when I shall relate all to thee! O Judas, what a fearful deed hast thou accomplished!

SCENE VIII.

CHRIST *in the midst of the Band of Men, sitting upon a chair.*

Servants (*one after another*). Is not this throne too mean for Thee, great King?—Hail to Thee, new-born Ruler! But sit more firmly, else mightest Thou perchance fall down. (*He pushes* JESUS *down.*)—Thou art verily also a Prophet. Then say, great Elias (*he strikes Him*), who is he that smote Thee?—Was it I? (*He also strikes Him.*)—Hearest Thou nothing? (*He shakes Him.*) Sleepest Thou?—He is deaf and dumb. A fine Prophet!—(*He pushes Him down from the chair so that He falls at full length.*) Alas, alas, our King has tumbled from His throne!—What is to be done now? we have no king left!—Thou art really to be pitied, Thou great Miracle-worker!—Come, let us help Him up again upon His throne!—(*They raise Him.*) Get up, mighty King! Receive anew our homage!

Messenger from Caiaphas (*entering*). Now, how goes it with the new King?

Band of Men. He speaks and prophesies not; we can do nothing with Him.

Messenger. The High Priest and Pilate will soon make Him speak. Caiaphas sends me to bring Him before him.

Selpha. Up, comrades!

Servant (*takes* JESUS *by the cords*). Get up, Thou hast been King long enough.

All. Away with Thee, Thy kingdom has come to an end!

ACT X.

THE DESPAIR OF JUDAS.

PROLOGUE.

Wherefore wanders Judas thus madly abroad? Alas! he is tortured by the pain of an evil conscience. Blood-guiltiness lies upon his soul, he roams about in fiery torment—the wages of sin. Weep, O Judas, for what thou hast committed! O blot out thy guilt with tears of penitence! In lowly hope entreat for grace! Yet doth the door of salvation stand open to thee. Woe, alas! Bitterest remorse tortures him indeed, but through the darkness no ray of hope shines on him. "Too great! too great is my sin!" he exclaims with Cain, the fratricide. Like him, comfortless and unrepentant, wild despair and horror seize upon him. That is the last wages of sin. This fate doth it urge on.

Chorus.

"O weh dem Menschen!" sprach der Herr
　"Der mich wird übergeben;
Es wäre besser ihm, wenn er
　Erhalten nie das Leben."

Und dieses Weh, das Jesus sprach,
·Folgt Judas auf dem Fusse nach.
In vollen Schaalen wird es sich ergiessen.
　Laut schreit um Rache das verkaufte Blut,
Gegeisselt von dem nagenden Gewissen,
　Gepeitscht von allen Furien der Wuth,

Rennt Judas rasend schon umher
Und findet keine Ruhe mehr.
Bis er, ach! von Verzweiflung fortgerissen
　Hinwirft von sich in wilder Hast
Des Lebens unerträglich schwere Last.

"Woe to that man," so spake the Lord,
　"By whom I am betray'd.
It had been better for that man
　If he had ne'er been born."

And now this woe, which Jesus spake,
　Follows on th' Iscariot's steps;
'Twill be poured out in measure full.
　The blood he sold for vengeance cries

Aloud :—by gnawing conscience scourg'd,
　Whipt by each Fury's frantic rage,

He now runs raving to and fro,
　And finds no rest for evermore.
Till he, alas! torn by despair, ·
　Casts from him in bewilder'd haste
The load intol'rable of life.

TABLEAU.—THE DEATH OF ABEL.

So flieht auch Kain. Ach, wohin!	Thus Cain too flies. Whither, alas!
Du kannst dir selbst doch nicht entflieh'n.	Thou canst not from thyself escape.
In dir trägst du die Höllenqual;	Thou bear'st within thee pains of hell;
Und eilest du von Ort zu Ort,	And hast'nest thou from place to place,
Sie schwingt die Geissel fort und fort.	Unceasingly the scourge is plied.
Wo du bist, ist sie überall;	Where'er thou art, the scourge is there;
Und nie entrinnst du deiner Pein.	Thou never canst outrun thy pain.
Diess soll der Sünder Spiegel sein;	This shall the sinners' mirror be;
Denn kommt die Rache heute nicht—	For if revenge come not to-day—
Wird noch dir Himmel borgen;	Yet Heaven on credit still can go;
So fällt das doppelte Gericht	So falls the double judgment sore
Auf ihre Häupter morgen.	Upon their heads the morrow morn.

SCENE I. (*See* p. 21.)

JUDAS *alone.*

My fearful foreboding has then become a horrible certainty, Caiaphas has condemned the Master to death and the Council has concurred in his judgment. It is over! no hope, no deliverance left. If the Master had willed to save Himself He would have made them feel His might a second time in the garden. Now He will do it no more. And what can I do for Him, I, miserable I, who have delivered Him into their hands? They shall have the money again—the blood money: they must give me my Master back again! Yet—will He be saved thereby? O vain hope! They will scorn me, I know it! Accursed synagogue! thou hast seduced me through thy messengers, hast hidden thy bloody design from me until thou hadst Him in thy clutches. I will have no part in the blood of the Innocent!   [*Exit.*

SCENE II.

The Sanhedrim.

Caiaphas. I thought, O fathers, that I could not wait till morning to send the Enemy of the synagogue to His death.

Annas. I also could get not a moment's rest, for eagerness to hear the judgment pronounced.

All. It is pronounced. He shall and must die!

Caiaphas. I will now have the Criminal brought in again in order that ye may all be convinced of His being guilty of death.

SCENE III.

JUDAS *hastening in.*

Judas. Is it true? Have ye condemned my Master to death?

Rabbi. Why dost thou force thyself in here unsummoned? Be off! Thou wilt be called if thou art wanted.

Judas. I must know it. Have ye condemned Him?

All. He must die!

Judas. Woe, woe, I have sinned! I have betrayed the Righteous! O ye, ye bloodthirsty judges, ye condemn and murder the guiltless!

All. Peace, Judas, or——

Judas. No peace for me for evermore! No peace for you! The blood of the Innocent cries for vengeance!

Caiaphas. What makes thee crazy? Speak, but speak with reverence. Thou standest before the Sanhedrim.

Judas. Ye are resolved to give Him up to death Who is pure from all guilt. Ye dare not! I protest against it! Ye have made me a traitor. Your accursed pieces of silver——

Annas. Thou didst thyself make the offer and conclude the bargain——

Priest. Recollect thyself, Judas! Thou hast received what thou didst desire. And if thou behavest thyself quietly, then mayest thou still——

Judas. I will have nothing more! I tear your shameful treaty in pieces! Give up the Innocent One!

Rabbi. Be off, madman!

Judas. I demand the Innocent One back again! My hand shall be pure from the blood——

Rabbi. What, thou infamous traitor, thou wilt prescribe laws to the Sanhedrim? Know this! Thy Master must die, and thou hast delivered Him to death.

All. He must die!

Judas (*with staring eyes*). Die? I am a traitor! (*Breaking out wildly.*) Then may ten thousand devils from hell tear me in pieces! May they grind me to powder! Here, ye bloodhounds, take your curse, your blood money! [*He throws down the bag.*

Caiaphas. Why didst thou let thyself be used for a transaction which thou hadst not weighed beforehand?

All. See thou to it.

Judas. Then my soul shall be damned, my body burst asunder, and ye——

All. Silence, and take thyself hence!

Judas. Ye shall be dragged with me into the abyss of hell!

[*He rushes out.*

SCENE IV.

Caiaphas (*after a pause*). A fearful man!

Annas. I had some foreboding of it.

Priest. It is his own fault.

Caiaphas. He has betrayed his Friend, we prosecute our Enemy. I stand fast in my resolve, and if there be one here who is of another mind, let him stand up.

All. No! What is determined, let it be carried out!

Caiaphas. What shall we do with this money? As blood money it may not be put into the treasury of God.

Priest. A burying-place for strangers is wanted. With this money a field for it could be bought.

Caiaphas. Is there such a one on sale?

Priest. A potter in the city has offered a piece of ground for sale, for just this price.

Caiaphas. Go then and buy it. But now we will no longer delay to pronounce the last sentence upon the Prisoner.

Rabbi. I will have Him immediately brought in.

Annas. I shall see whether the scorn which He showed towards me has yet left Him. It will be a true satisfaction to me to have a voice in the sentence—Let Him die.

SCENE V.

CHRIST *before the Sanhedrim.*

Selpha (*bringing in* JESUS). Reverence the Council better than before.

Caiaphas. Lead Him into the midst.

Balbus. Stand forth! (*He pushes the Prisoner forwards.*)

Caiaphas. Jesus of Nazareth, dost Thou persist in the words which Thou this night hast spoken before Thy judges?

Annas. If Thou art the Christ, tell us.

Christ. If I tell you, ye will not believe: and if I also ask you, ye will not answer me, nor let me go. Hereafter shall the Son of man sit on the right hand of the power of God.

All. Art Thou then the Son of God?

Christ. Ye say that I am.

Annas. It is enough. What need we any further witness?

Priests and Pharisees (*who were not present at the night Council*). We have now heard of His own mouth.

Caiaphas. Fathers of the people of Israel! it behoves you now to determine the final sentence as to the guilt and the punishment of this Man.

All. He is guilty of blasphemy! He hath deserved death!

Caiaphas. We will accordingly lead Him before the judgment-seat of Pilate.

All. Yea, away with Him! Let Him die!

Caiaphas. Pilate must, however, be first informed about the matter in order that he may publish the sentence before the feast. (*He sends a Rabbi and two other members of the Council to* PILATE.) This day will indeed save the religion of our fathers and exalt the honour of the synagogue, so that the echo of our renown may resound to our latest descendants. Lead Him away, we follow!

All. Death to the Galilæan!

SCENE VI.

The Three Messengers of the Sanhedrim before PILATE'S *House.*

Rabbi. At length we breathe more freely, we have been insulted long enough.

First Priest. It was full time, His following is already very large.

Rabbi. Now there is nothing more to fear from Him. The traders have to-day shown the most praiseworthy activity, in order to gain for us a crowd of determined folk. Ye will see: if it comes to anything, these will give the tone decidedly. The weak-minded will consent with them, and the followers of the Nazarene will find it well to be silent, and to withdraw themselves.

First Priest. How shall we bring our request before Pilate? We must not enter the house of the heathen to-day else we shall be unclean to eat the Passover.

Rabbi. We will have the petition delivered through his people (*knocks at the door. To* PILATE'S *Servant, who comes out*) The High Priest sends us to petition the sublime representative of Cæsar that he would permit the Council to appear before him, and to bring a Criminal before him for ratification of His sentence.

Servant. I will at once give the message. [*Exit.*

First Priest. It is sad that we must knock at a heathen's door in order to fulfil the claims of the holy law.

Rabbi. Courage! When once our domestic Enemy is out of the way, who knows if we shall not soon get rid of this stranger?

Second Priest. O that I could see the day which will bring freedom to the children of Israel!

Servant (*returning*). The Governor greets you. You are to announce to the High Priests that Pilate is ready to receive the petition of the San-hedrim.

Rabbi. Accept our thanks.

Second Priest (as they are going). Pilate will surely assent to the demand of the Sanhedrim ?

Rabbi. He must! How can he stand out when the Sanhedrim and the whole people require the death of this Man ?

First Priest. What does the life of a Galilæan matter to the Governor ? Even to please the High Priest, which is worth much to him, he will not hesitate to allow the execution. [*Exeunt.*

SCENE VII. (*See* p. 22.)

The End of JUDAS. *A Woody Scene.*

Judas. Whither shall I go to hide my infamy ? No forest darkness is secret enough, no rocky cavern deep enough! Swallow me up, O earth! Alas, my Master, best of all men, have I sold—delivered Him up to ill-treatment, to the most agonizing death! How gracious was He even towards me! How He comforted me when gloomy misery often oppressed my soul! How lovingly did He remind me and warn me, even when already I brooded over my treachery! Execrable covetousness, thou alone hast seduced me! Alas, now no longer a disciple, never dare I again come into the presence of one of the brethren! An outcast—everywhere hated and abhorred even by those who led me astray—I wander about alone with this glowing fire in my heart! Alas, if I could only dare again to behold His countenance, I might cling to Him, the only Anchor of hope! but He lies in prison, is perchance already put to death through the fury of His enemies—ah no! through my guilt! Woe is me—me, the offscouring of mankind! For me there is no hope, my crime can no longer be repaired by any penitence! He is dead, and I am His murderer! Unhappy hour, when my mother bore me! Shall I any longer bear these tortures? No, I will not go a step further! Here will I breathe thee out, accursed life! Let the most miserable of all fruit hang on this tree! (*He tears off his girdle.*) Ha! come, thou serpent, twist round me! strangle the traitor!

[*He prepares for suicide. The curtain falls.*

ACT XI.

CHRIST BEFORE PILATE.

PROLOGUE.

Hardly were the words heard, " Death to Him, the Enemy of Moses!" than they are taken up by many voices. Thirsting with tiger-thirst for the Gentile sentence, ye gather tumultuously together, take counsel unwearyingly, bring accusation upon accusation, impatiently expecting the sentence of condemnation. So once against Daniel the thousand-voiced cry arose, " He has destroyed Baal! Away with him to the lions' den! He shall be their prey!" Alas! when deceiving misconceptions have found entrance into the human heart, man is no longer himself. Injustice becomes to him virtue, whilst he hates and fights against virtue.

Chorus.

" Gelästert hat er Gott !
Wir brauchen keine Zeugen mehr.
 Verdammt zum Tod
 Ist vom Gesetze er ;"
So lärmet das Synedrium.
"Auf! zu Pilatus wollen wir,
Ihm unsere Klagen vorzubringen—
Das Todesurtheil zu erzwingen."

" He hath blasphemed God !
We need no witness more.
 Condemned to death
 By law is He";—
So rages the Sanhedrim.
" Up ! we will hence to Pilate,
Bring our complaints before him,
Sentence of death force from him."

TABLEAU.—DANIEL ACCUSED BEFORE DARIUS.

In diesem stummen Bilde sehet ihr :
Wie Daniel zu Babylon,
Verklagt man fälschlich Gottes Sohn.

Look well on this dumb picture :—
As Daniel erst at Babylon,
God's Son they falsely now accuse.

" Der Götter Feind ist Daniel !
O König ! höre deiner Völker Klagen :
Zerstört hat er den grossen Bel—
Die Priester und den Drachen er erschlagen.
Ergrimmt vor deinem Thron
Erscheint ganz Babylon.

" Foe of the gods is Daniel !
O King, hear thou thy people's plaint :
Great Bel hath he destroyed—
The priests and dragon hath he slain.
Furious before thy throne
Appears all Babylon.

Willst du von Volkes Wuth dich retten ;
So lass den Feind der Götter tödten.
 Er sterbe !—König ! nur sein Tod
 Versöhnet unsern grossen Gott."

The people's wrath wilt thou escape ?
Then give to death the gods' great foe.
 Death to him ! Death alone, O King,
 Will reconcile our gods to us."

So eilt das böse Sanhedrin
Ganz rasend zu Pilatus hin,
 Wie jene Schurken dort gethan ;

So hastes the wicked Sanhedrim
In furious rage to Pilate,
 E'en as those wretches once had done;

Und klagt mit wildem Ungestüm,	And with wild tumult they make suit,
Voll Tigerwuth und Löwengrimm,	With tiger's rage and lion's wrath,
Die Unschuld auf den Tod nun an.	That Innocence to death be brought.
O Neid! satanisches Gezücht,	O Envy! Satan's offspring vile,
Was unternimmst, was wagst du nicht,	What wilt thou not begin—or dare,
Um deinen Groll zu stillen?	To satisfy thy rancorous spite?
Nichts ist dir heilig, nichts zu gut;	To thee nought holy is, or good;
Du opferst Alles deiner Wuth	All thou dost sacrifice to rage,
Und deinem bösen Willen.	And to thy wicked will.
Weh dem, den diese Leidenschaft	Woe to him whom this passion fierce
In Schlangenketten mit sich rafft!—	Draws to itself with serpent-chains!
Vor neidischen Gelüsten,	'Gainst envious desires,
O Brüder! bleibet auf der Hut!	O brothers, be upon your guard!
Nie lasset diese Natterbrut	Nor ever let this viper-brood
In euren Busen nisten!	Nestle within your hearts.

SCENE I. (*See* pp. 22, 23.)

Before PILATE'S *House. On the left the Sanhedrim, the Traders and Witnesses; on the right the Band of Men with* JESUS.

Band of Men (bringing JESUS *forward)*. Away with Thee to death, false Prophet!—Ha! Doth it terrify Thee, that Thou wilt not come forward?

Selpha. Drive Him on!

Band of Men. Must we carry Thee in our arms?—Get on! Thy journey will not last much longer!—Only out to Calvary! There, on the Cross, canst thou comfortably rest!

Caiaphas. Be quiet! We wish to have ourselves announced. (*They are quiet.*) Ye members of the Sanhedrim! If the holy teaching inherited by us, if our honour, if the peace of the whole land be still dear to you, then consider well this moment! It decides between us and that Deceiver! If ye be men in whose veins still flows the blood of your fathers, then hear us! An imperishable monument will ye set up for yourselves. Be firm in your resolve!

The Sanhedrim. Long live our fathers! Death to the Enemy of our nation!

Caiaphas. Do not rest till He be blotted out of the number of the living!

All. We will not rest!

Band of Men. Hearest Thou, O King, O Prophet?

SCENE II.

PILATE *appears with Attendants upon his Balcony.*

Caiaphas (bowing). Viceroy of the great Emperor of Rome!

All. Health and blessings attend thee!

Caiaphas. We have brought a Man, by name Jesus, here before thy judgment-seat, that thou mayest have executed the sentence of death pronounced upon Him by the Sanhedrim.

Pilate. Bring Him forth. What accusations bring ye against this Man?

Caiaphas. If He were not a malefactor, we would not have delivered Him up unto thee, but would have punished Him ourselves according to the order of our law.

Pilate. Now—what evil deeds hath He committed?

Caiaphas. He hath in manifold ways gravely offended against the holy law of Israel.

Pilate. Then take ye Him and judge Him according to your law.

Annas. He hath already been judged by the Sanhedrim and declared guilty of death.

All the Priests. For according to our law He hath deserved death.

Caiaphas. But it is not lawful for us to put any man to death. Therefore bring we the demand for the fulfilment of the sentence before the Viceroy of the Emperor.

Pilate. How can I deliver a man to death without I know his crime, and before I have convinced myself that the crime is worthy of death? What hath He done?

Rabbi. The judgment of the Council against this man was given with one voice, and grounded upon an exact examination of His crime. Therefore it does not seem necessary that the noble Governor should give himself the trouble of a second inquiry.

Pilate. What? Ye dare to suggest to me, who stand in the Emperor's place, that I should be a blind tool for the execution of your resolve? That be far from me! I must know what law He hath transgressed, and in what manner.

Caiaphas. We have a law, and by our law He ought to die, because He made Himself the Son of God.

Annas. Therefore must we insist that He suffer the lawful punishment of death.

Pilate. On account of such a speech, which at worst is only the dream of a fanciful imagination, a Roman can find no one guilty of death. Who knows, too, if this Man be not the Son of some god? If you have no other crime to lay to His charge do not expect that I shall fulfil your desire.

Caiaphas. Not merely against our holy law, but also against the

Emperor himself has this Man been guilty of grave crimes. We have found Him an insurgent and a deceiver of the people.

All. He stirreth up the people ; He is a rebel !

Pilate. I have indeed heard of One Jesus Who goeth about the land and teacheth and doeth marvellous works ; but never have I heard of any insurrection stirred up by Him. If anything of the sort had happened, I should have known it before you, since I am placed in this country for the administration of peace, and am perfectly informed concerning the doings and practices of the Jews. But say : when and where did He stir up an insurrection ?

Nathanael. He brings troops of people in thousands around Him, and just a short time ago, surrounded by such a crowd, He made a solemn entry into Jerusalem itself.

Pilate. I know it, but nothing seditious was caused by it.

Caiaphas. Is it not sedition when He forbids the people to give tribute to Cæsar ?

Pilate. Where is your proof ?

Caiaphas. Proof sufficient, since He gives Himself out for the Messiah, the King of Israel ! Is not that a challenge for the downfall of the Emperor ?

Pilate. I marvel at your suddenly-aroused zeal for the authority of Cæsar. (*To* CHRIST) Hearest Thou what heavy complaints these bring against Thee ? What answerest Thou ?   [CHRIST *is silent.*

Caiaphas. See ! He cannot deny it.

Priest. His silence is a confession of His crime.

All (*making a tumult*). Sentence Him, then !

Pilate. Patience ! there is time enough for that. I will take Him apart for a private hearing. (*To his Attendants*) Perchance, when He is no longer affrighted by the crowd and the fury of His accusers, He will speak and answer me. Let Him be brought into the porch. (*To the Servant.*) Go ; my soldiers will take charge of Him. (*To the Members of the Council*) And ye—consider once again the ground, or want of ground, for your complaints, and examine well whether they do not ·perchance spring from an impure source. Let me then know your sentiments.

[*Turns away from them.*

Rabbi (*going away*). This is a troublesome delay.

Caiaphas. Do not lose courage. Victory belongs to the steadfast !

SCENE III.

PILATE *and Attendants.* CHRIST *is brought forth upon the Balcony.*

Pilate (*to* CHRIST). Thou hast heard the accusation of the Council against Thee. Give me an answer thereto ! Thou hast, they say, called Thyself the Son of God. Whence art Thou ? (CHRIST *is silent.*)

Speakest Thou not unto me? Knowest Thou not that I have power to crucify Thee, and have power to release Thee?

Christ. Thou couldst have no power at all against me except it were given thee from above. Therefore he that delivered me unto thee hath the greater sin.

Pilate (aside). Frankly spoken! (*To* CHRIST) Art Thou the King of the Jews?

Christ. Sayest thou this thing of thyself, or did others tell it thee of me?

Pilate. Am I a Jew? Thine own nation and the chief Priests have delivered Thee unto me. They accuse Thee, that Thou hast desired to be the King of Israel. What hast Thou done?

Christ. My kingdom is not of this world. If my kingdom were of this world, then would my servants fight, that I should not be delivered to the Jews; but now is my kingdom not from hence.

Pilate. Art Thou a King, then?

Christ. Thou sayest it. I am a King. To this end was I born, and for this cause came I into the world, that I should bear witness unto the truth. Every one that is of the truth heareth my voice.

Pilate. What is truth?

SCENE IV.

Enter Servant of PILATE.

Servant. My lord, thy consort greeteth thee, and earnestly prays thee for the sake of thine own and her welfare that thou wouldst have nothing to do with that just Man, Who has been accused before thy judgment-seat. She has suffered anguish and terror this night in a fearful dream because of Him.

Pilate. Go hence and tell her that she may be without anxiety. I will take no part in the attempts of the Jews, but rather do everything to save Him.

SCENE V.

Pilate (to his Attendants). I would that I knew nothing of this matter. What think ye, my friends, of the complaints of the Jewish priests?

First Courtier. They are only impelled by envy and jealousy. The most passionate hatred expresses itself in their words and their mien.

Second Courtier. The hypocrites pose as though they had the authority of the Emperor much at heart, while there is no question except of their own authority, which they believe endangered through this famous Teacher of the people.

Pilate. I think as you do. I cannot believe that this Man hath any criminal plans in His mind. There is something so noble in His features and His demeanour,—His words also exhibit such noble frankness and high endowments, that He appears to me to be far more a very wise Man, perchance too wise, for these gloomy men to bear the light of His wisdom.—And the sorrowful dream of my consort concerning Him?—If perchance He were truly of a higher origin?—No! I will by no means permit myself to meet the wishes of the priesthood. (*To the Servant*) Let the High Priest again appear here,—and let the Accused be again led from the judgment-hall. [*Exit the Servant.*

SCENE VI.

The same. The Sanhedrim under the Balcony.

Pilate. Here ye have your Prisoner again. He is without fault.

Annas. We have the Emperor's word that our law shall be uprightly maintained. How can He be found without guilt who trod under foot this same law?

All. He is guilty of death!

Caiaphas. Is He not also punishable by the Emperor when He has maliciously injured that which the Emperor's will has secured to us?

Pilate. I have told you already: if He hath committed anything against your law, then punish Him according to your law, so far as ye are authorized thereto. I cannot pronounce the sentence of death upon Him because I find nothing in him which, after the law by which I have to judge Him, deserveth death.

Caiaphas. If any one giveth himself out as a king, is he not a rebel? Doth he not deserve the punishment of high treason—the punishment of death?

Pilate. If this Man hath called Himself a King, this ambiguous word merely doth not justify me in condemning Him. With us it is openly taught that every wise man is a king. But ye have brought forward no facts as to His usurping kingly power.

Nathanael. Is it not fact enough when He stirreth up the people, teaching throughout all Jewry, beginning from Galilee, where He first gathered followers together, to this place.

Pilate. Hath He come out of Galilee?

All. Yea, He is a Galilæan.

Rabbi. His home is Nazareth, in King Herod's jurisdiction.

Pilate. If that be so, I am spared the office of judge. Herod, the King of Galilee, has come hither to the Feast; he may now judge his subject. Take Him away, and bring Him to His king. He shall be conducted by my body-guard. [*Exit with his Attendants.*

Caiaphas. Away, then, to Herod! With him who professes himself of the faith of our fathers shall we find better protection for our holy law.

All (*to* CHRIST). An hour sooner or later! But Thou must come to it. To-day also! [*Exeunt omnes.*

ACT XII. (*See* p. 23.)

CHRIST *before* HEROD.

PROLOGUE.

He, the most loving, meets with fresh outrages before Herod, because He does not flatteringly exercise the gifts of a seer before that vain prince, or work miracles. Therefore is Wisdom Itself by fools despised as a fool, and, arrayed in a white garment, set forth as a spectacle for a short time to the mocking servants of the king. Samson, the dread hero-youth, now bereft of eyesight and fettered, is laughed at and despised for His weakness by the Philistines. Yet, He who now seems weak will show forth strength. He who seems cast down will shine forth in greatness. Above worthless scorn Virtue reigns sublime.

Chorus.

Vergebens sprühet vor des Richters Schranken	In vain within the judgment-hall shoots forth
Erboster Hass der Lästrung Flammenglut.	Wild hate, the glowing flames of calumny.
Der Richtertritt entgegen ohne Wanken ;	To meet them comes the judge unwavering ;
An seiner Feste bricht der Feinde Wuth.	The foe's wrath breaks upon his steadfastness.
Doch ruht sie nicht !—Bekümmert gehen Wir Jesu zu Herodes nach.	Yet rest they not !—Sadly we must follow Jesus to Herod.
Dort—ach !—betrübten Herzens sehen Wir Ihm bereitet neue Schmach.	There, ah, with mournful hearts we see Fresh shame prepared for Him.

TABLEAU.—SAMSON MAKING SPORT FOR THE PHILISTINES.

Chorus.

Seht Samson : Seht die starke Hand— Sie muss der Knechtschaft Fessel tragen ! Der Held, der Tausende geschlagen— Er trägt des Sklaven Spottgewand !	See Samson : See how the strong hand The chains of slavery must bear ! The hero, who a thousand slew, Slave's garb of scorn he now must wear.
Den Feinden einst so fürchterlich Dient er zu ihres Hohnes Ziele ; Philister brauchen ihn zum Spiele, Erfreu'n an seiner Schwäche sich.	So dreadful once to enemies, He serves as aim for all their scorn ; Philistines use him for their sport, Rejoice themselves in his decay.
So steht auch Jesus, Gottes Sohn, Zu stolzer Thoren Augenweide, Geschmäht, verlacht im weissen Kleide, Und überhäuft mit Spott und Hohn.	Thus also Jesu, God's Son, stands, The gazing-stock of haughty fools, Revil'd, derided, in white robes, And overwhelm'd with spite and scorn.

SCENE I.

A Hall.—HEROD *and his Court.*

Herod. So they have the renowned Magician Jesus of Nazareth as Prisoner with them. Of a long season have I been desirous to see Him of whose works so much is spoken. I will prove His miraculous power.

Courtier. He will surely be willingly ready, O King, to show forth His works to thee in order to gain thy favour against His accusers.

Herod. They may bring their accusations before Pilate; I have nothing to examine here, and nothing to pronounce.

Courtier. Perchance the Governor has sent them away, and now they seek to attain their end in another way.

Herod. I will not meddle with their pious squabbles, I will only see Him and prove His miraculous powers.

SCENE II.

The same.—CAIAPHAS, ANNAS, PRIESTS.—CHRIST *led by Soldiers.*

Caiaphas. Most mighty king!

All the Priests. Hail and blessing!

Caiaphas. The Sanhedrim has seized a Seducer and brings Him before the king for confirmation of the lawful punishment.

Herod. How can I give judgment in a foreign territory? . . . (*To* CHRIST) Give us a proof of Thy learning, we will then together with the people honour Thee and believe on Thee.

Priests. O King, let not thyself be led astray! He is in covenant with Beelzebub.

Herod. It is the same to me. Tell me, what did I dream last night? (CHRIST *is silent.*) Perchance Thou canst interpret to me my dream. (*He relates it.* CHRIST *answers not.*) Thou art not well skilled in this line of business? Then cause that this hall may suddenly become dark, change that roll there, which contains Thy sentence, into a serpent! (*To his Courtiers*) He knows nothing and can do nothing. He is a fool, whom the applause of the people has made crazy. (*To the* PRIESTS) Let Him go!

Caiaphas. O King, trust Him not! He only pretends to be a fool in order to get a mild sentence from thee by artifice.

Annas. Even the person of the king is in danger, for He has given Himself out as a King.

Herod. He! As a King? As a King of fools! As such He deserves homage, therefore will I give Him a king's robe and formally install Him as King of fools.   [*He makes a sign to a servant.*

Priests. Not so, He hath deserved death!

Caiaphas. O King, think upon thy duty to punish the transgressor of the law!

H

Herod. What have ye exactly against Him?

Rabbi. He hath profaned the Sabbath!

Nathanael. He hath blasphemed God!

Priest. He hath declared that He will destroy the Temple, and in three days will build it up.

Herod. Well, He hath rightly proved Himself a King of fools.

Priest. He hath so far presumed, O King, as to call thee a fox.

Herod. Then has He laid to my door a quality which entirely suits Himself. (*A Servant comes with a robe.*) Array Him! Thus shall He play His part amongst the people.

Priests. He shall die!

Herod. No, I will not shed the blood of so exalted a King. Bring Him before the people, that they may marvel at Him to their hearts' desire.   [*The Soldiers lead* JESUS *away amidst mocking words.*

SCENE III.

Caiaphas. Thou seest now, O King, that His mighty works are nothing but lies and deceit, by which He has seduced the people; give then thy sentence.

Herod. My sentence is: He is a simple fellow, and not capable of the crime of which ye accuse Him.

Caiaphas. O King, give heed that thou deccive not thyself.

Herod. One must deal with fools as fools. My court of justice is over.

Rabbi. So this has come to pass concerning the law, Moses, and the prophets!

Herod. I hold by my sentence. I am weary, and will no longer meddle with the story. Pilate may decide according to the duty of his office. Offer him greeting and friendly salutation from King Herod.

[*Exeunt the* PRIESTS.

SCENE IV.

Herod. I was mistaken. Instead of a worker of miracles, I found a quite ordinary man.

Courtier. How doth lying report know how to embellish things!

Herod. Friend, that is no John. John spake with a wisdom and power which one was forced to esteem, but this Man is as dumb as a fish.

Courtier. I am only surprised at the bitter hatred of the Priests against Him.

Herod. If Pilate had found Him a State Criminal he would not have sent Him to me; but enough of this wearisome matter, we will make amends for lost time by better entertainment.

ACT XIII.

The Scourging and Crown of Thorns.

PROLOGUE.

Alas! what a sight here presents itself to our eyes, ever to be contemplated by the disciples of Christ! The body of the Lord wounded all over with innumerable blows of the scourge, His head crowned with a sharp, thorny wreath! His countenance scarcely recognizable, running down with blood! who would not here shed a tear of inmost pity? When our father Jacob beheld the bloody coat of his beloved how did he tremble and weep, full of sorrow, giving way to heartrending cries of grief! Let us also weep when we see the Divine Friend of our soul endure such things, for ah! on account of our sins is He wounded and torn.

Chorus.

Sie haben noch nicht ausgewüthet—	Not yet have they from raging ceas'd—
Nicht ist der Rache Durst gestillt	Their thirst for vengeance is not still'd ;
Nur über Mordgedanken brütet	Only on thoughts of murder broods
Die Schaar, von Satans Groll erfüllt.	The band, with Satan's hatred fill'd.
Kann diese Herzen denn nichts mehr erweichen?	Can nought e'er soften then these hearts?
Auch nicht ein Leib, zerfleischt von Geisselstreichen,	Not e'en a body, torn by scourge-strokes,
Mit Wunden ohne Zahl bedeckt?	Cover'd with wounds innum'rable?
Ist nichts, was noch ein Mitleid weckt?	Can sympathy by nought be waked?

FIRST TABLEAU.—JOSEPH'S BRETHREN BRINGING HIS BLOODY COAT TO JACOB.

Chorus.

O! welche schaudervolle Scene,	O, what a scene of horror dire !
Des Josephs Rock mit Blut besprengt	The coat of Joseph stained with blood,
Und an den Wangen Jacobs hängt	And Jacob's aged cheeks are wet
Der tiefsten Trauer heisse Thräne.	With bitter tears of deepest grief.
"Wo ist mein Joseph? meine Wonne !	"Where is my Joseph? where my joy,
An dessen Aug' mein Auge ruht.	In whose sweet eyes mine eyes find rest?
An diesem Rocke hängt das Blut,	The blood is dripping from this coat,
Das Blut von Joseph—meinem Sohne.	The blood of Joseph—of my son.
Ein wildes Thier hat ihn zerrissen,	A wild beast must have mangled him,
Zerrissen meinen Liebling. Ach !	Torn him, my darling. Ah, alas !
Dir will ich nach—dir, Joseph ! nach;	Thee, Joseph, will I follow soon ;
Kein Trost kann diess mein Leid versüssen."	My pain no comfort can assuage."

H 2

So jammert er—so wimmert er
   Um Joseph—und er ist nicht mehr.
So wird auch Jesu Leib zerrissen
   Mit wilder Wuth,
   Sein kostbar Blut
In Strömen aus den Wunden fliessen.

Thus mourns he—thus doth he lament
   For Joseph—that he is no more.
Thus Jesu's body will be torn
   With wildest rage,
   His Precious Blood
In streams from every wound will flow.

SECOND TABLEAU.--THE SACRIFICE OF ISAAC.

"Abraham ! Abraham ! tödt' ihn nicht.
Dein Glaube hat"—so spricht
Jehova—"ihn, den Einzigen gegeben :
Er soll nun wieder dein—zum Völker-
   Glücke leben."

"Abraham ! Abraham ! slay him not
Thy faith hath "—thus saith
Jehovah—"giv'n up thine only son :
Thine now again—for nations' weal shall
   live."

Und Abra'm sah im Dorngesträuch
   Verwickelt einen Wider steh'n ;
Er nahm, und opferte sogleich
   Ihn, von Jehova ausersehn.

Within the thicket Abr'am saw
A ram caught in the thorny shoots,
He took and quickly offered it,
Jehovah's chosen sacrifice.

Ein gross Geheimniss zeigt diess Bild
Im heil'gen Dunkel noch verhüllt.
Wie dieses Opfer einst auf Moria,
Steht Jesus bald gekrönt mit Dörnern da.

This type shows a great mystery
Still veiled in holy twilight gloom.
As once Moriah's sacrifice,
With thorns crown'd Christ will soon
   appear.

Der Dornbekrönte wird für uns sein Leben,
Wie es der Vater will, zum Opfer geben.
   Wo trifft man eine Liebe an,
   Die dieser Liebe gleichen kann?

The Thorn-Crown'd will for us His life
An off'ring give—the Father's Will.
   Where can we ever find a love
   Which to this Love can equal be?

SCENE I. (*See* p. 24.)

(*See* p. 24.)

CAIAPHAS, ANNAS, *the* COUNCIL, *the* TRADERS *and the Witnesses appear
again, with* CHRIST *led by Soldiers, before* PILATE'S *House.*

Caiaphas. Now must we the more importunately challenge Pilate, and
if he does not judge after our will then shall the authority of the Emperor
force the sentence from him.

Annas. Shall I now in my old age see the synagogue destroyed ?
But no ! with stammering tongue will I call for blood and death upon this
Criminal, and then descend to my father's sepulchre if I can see this
Malefactor die upon the cross.

Rabbi. We will sooner allow ourselves to be buried beneath the ruins
of the Temple than go back from our resolve.

Pharisees. We must not give it up until He be given up to death.

Caiaphas. He who does not stand by this resolution, let him be put
out of the synagogue.

Annas. Let the curse of our fathers light upon Him !

Caiaphas. Time presses, the day wears on, now must all means be
employed that even to-day before the feast our will be accomplished.

SCENE II.

PILATE *appears with Attendants upon the Balcony.*

Caiaphas. We bring the Prisoner once more before thy judgment-seat, and earnestly require His death.

Priests and Pharisees. We insist upon it! He must die!

Pilate. Ye have brought this Man unto me as one that perverteth the people ; and, behold, I, having examined Him before you, have found no fault in this Man touching those things whereof ye accuse Him.

Caiaphas. We stand by our accusation. He is a Criminal worthy of death!

Priests. A Criminal against our law and against the Emperor.

Pilate. Because He is a Galilæan, I have sent him to Herod. Have ye then brought forward your accusations?

Caiaphas. Yea, Herod would decide nothing, because here thou art in authority.

Pilate. He also found nothing worthy of death in Him, therefore, in order to meet your demands, I will cause this Man to be chastised with scourging ; but then release Him.

Annas. That sufficeth not!

Caiaphas. The law doth not award to such a Criminal the punishment of scourging, but that of death.

Priests. To death with Him!

Pilate. Is your hatred against this Man so deep and bitter that it cannot be satisfied by blood from His wounds? Ye force me to say openly to you that which I think. Moved by ignoble passion, ye persecute Him, because the people are better inclined to Him than to you. I have long enough heard your hateful accusations, I will now hear the voice of the people. A countless multitude will soon assemble here, in order, after ancient custom, to request the release of a prisoner at the feast of the Passover. Then will it be shown whether your accusations are the expression of the people's mind or only of your personal hatred.

Caiaphas (bowing). It will be shown, O Governor, that thou unjustly thinkest evil of us.

Priest. Truly, not hatred but holy zeal for the law of God is it which moves us to desire His death.

Pilate. Ye know of the murderer Barabbas, who lies in fetters, and of his evil deeds. I will give the people the choice between him and Jesus of Nazareth. Him whom they desire, him will I release.

All. Release Barabbas unto us and crucify Jesus.

Pilate. Ye are not the people, the people will speak for themselves, meanwhile I will chastise Him. (*To a Servant*) Let the soldiers lead Him away and scourge Him after the Roman law. (*To those around him*) Whatsoever He hath done amiss will thereby be sufficiently expiated, and perchance the sight of the Scourged One may mitigate the wrath of His enemies. [*Exit with Attendants.*

SCENE III. *(See p. 25.)*

The PRIESTS, *etc., beneath the empty Balcony.*

Caiaphas. Pilate appeals to the voice of the people. Good, we will appeal to the same. (*To the* TRADERS *and* WITNESSES) Now, gallant Israelites, your time has come. Go hence into the streets of Jerusalem and summon your friends to come hither. Bring them together in a close band! Inflame them with the most fiery hatred against the Enemy of Moses. Seek to win the weak-minded by the power of your words, and by promises. Terrify the followers of the Galilæan by a united outcry against them, by insult and storm, and, if it must be, through ill-treatment, so that none of them may dare to let themselves be seen here, much less to open their mouths.

Traders and Witnesses. We will hasten hence and quickly return, each one at the head of an inflamed troop.

Caiaphas. We will all assemble in the street of the Sanhedrim.

[*Exeunt the* TRADERS. *The* PRIESTS *call after them :* Hail, true disciples of Moses !

Caiaphas. Let us now not delay a moment! Let us go to meet the different bands to encourage them, and to inflame them!

Annas. From all the streets of Jerusalem we will then bring the assembled people before the judgment-hall.

Rabbi. Since Pilate wishes to hear the voice of the people, let him hear it !

Caiaphas. Let him hear the cry of the nation with one voice. Release unto us Barabbas, and crucify the Galilæan!

All. Release unto us Barabbas, and crucify the Galilæan ! [*Exeunt.*

SCENE IV.

CHRIST *stripped of His Garments, and His Hands bound to a low Pillar, around Him the Soldiers.*

Soldiers (*one after another*). Now hath He enough, He is all running down with blood!—Thou poor King of the Jews!—But what a King is that? He bears no sceptre in His hand, no crown upon His head ?—That can be mended. I will at once fetch the ensigns of the Jewish kingdom. (*He brings a purple robe, the crown of thorns, and the reed.*) Here! that is truly a most fair adornment for the King of the Jews! Thou didst not expect such honour, didst Thou ?—Come, let the purple robe fall around Thee ; but sit down, a King must not stand. And here is a fine pointed crown ! (*They put it on Him.*) Show Thyself! (*Laughter.*) In order, however, that it fall not from His head, it must be firmly set on. Here, brothers, help me! (*Four Soldiers take hold of the ends of two staves and press down the crown.* CHRIST *shrinks in pain.*) Here is the sceptre!—Now nothing more is wanting to Thee.—What a King! (*They kneel before Him.*) Hail, Mighty King of the Jews!

Servant of Pilate (*coming in*). The Prisoner must immediately be brought to the judgment-hall.

Soldiers. Thou comest at a wrong time, thou hast disturbed us in the midst of our marks of reverence. Get up! They want to carry Thee about for a show. There will be rejoicing amongst the people of the Jews when their King appears before them in fullest pomp.

[*Exeunt with* JESUS.

ACT XIV. (*See p. 25.*)

JESUS *condemned to Death.*

PROLOGUE.

The Redeemer stands forth an Image of sorrow. Himself moved with compassion, Pilate brings Him forth. Hast thou then no pity, O befooled, deceived people? No! Seized with madness, they cry, Crucify Him! They demand torture and death for the Holiest and pardon for the murderer Barabbas. O how differently did Joseph once stand before the people of Egypt! Songs of gladness and jubilation sounded in his ears; he was solemnly installed as the saviour of Egypt. But around Him, the Saviour of the world, rages a deceived people, who rest not and cease not until the judge unwillingly pronounces: Take ye Him and crucify Him.

Chorus.

Ach seht den König! seht zum Hohne	O see the King! See Him in scorn
Gekrönt ihn! ach, mit welcher Krone!	As monarch-crown'd—with what a crown!
Und welch ein Scepter in der Hand!	And with what sceptre in his hand!
Mit Purpur seht ihr ihn behangen;	See Him in purple robe array'd,
Ach ja! im rothen Lappen prangen.	Yea, and with crimson rays bedeck'd.
Ist das des Königs Festgewand? .	Is that the festal garb of Kings?
Wo ist an ihm der Gottheit Spur?	Where is in Him the Godhead's mark?
Ach! welch ein Mensch!	Behold the Man!
Ein Wurm—ein Spott der Henker nur.	A worm—the scorn of hangmen now.

FIRST TABLEAU.—JOSEPH MADE GOVERNOR OVER EGYPT.

Seht! welch ein Mensch!—	Behold the man!
Zur Hoheit Joseph auserwählt	Joseph is called to dignity—
Seht! welch ein Mensch!—	Behold the man!
Zum Mitleid Jesu vorgestellt.	Jesu brought forth for sympathy.

Laut soll es durch Aegypten schallen :
  Es lebe Joseph hoch und hehr !
Und tausendfach soll's wiederhallen :
  Aegyptens Vater—Freund ist er !
Und Alles stimme—gross und klein—
  In unsern frohen Jubel ein !

Loud shall it ring through Egypt's coasts :
  " Live Joseph long ! both high and great !"
A thousand times shall it resound :
  " Father of Egypt !—friend to all ! "
And all unite, both great and small,
  In our triumphant jubilee.

Du bist Aegyptens Trost und Freude,
  Ein Glück wie ihm noch keines war.
Dir, Joseph, bringt Aegypten heute
  Die Huldigung voll Jubel dar.
Laut soll es durch Aegypten schallen (*wie oben*).

Of Egypt thou the stay and joy,
  And blessing, such as ne'er has been.
Joseph, to-day doth Egypt bring
  Her homage full of joy to Thee.
Loud shall it ring through Egypt's coasts,
  &c.

Als zweiter Landesvater thronet
  Er nun in uns'rer Mitt und Brust !
Der Herbes uur mit Segen lohnet—
  Ihm Heil ! des Landes Stolz und Lust.
Laut soll es durch Aegypten schallen (*wie oben*).

The country's second father, he
  Now reigns within our realm and hearts !
E'en the perverse with blessing pays—
  Hail to him ! Egypt's pride and joy !
Loud shall it ring through Egypt's coasts,
  &c.

SECOND TABLEAU.—THE GOAT SACRIFICED AS A SIN-OFFERING.

Chorus.

Des alten Bundes Opfer diess,
Wie es Jehova bringen liess :
Zwei Böcke wurden vorgestellt,
Darüber dann das Loos gefällt,
Wen sich Jehova auserwählt.
  Jehova, durch das Opferblut
  Sei deinem Volke wieder gut.

The ancient cov'nant's off'ring this,
As God ordain'd it should be brought.
Two goats before His altar placed,
And then on one the lot doth fall—
The one by God chos'n for Himself.
  Jehovah ! through blood-offering
  Again be to Thy people good !

Das Blut der Böcke will der Herr
Im neuen Bunde nimmermehr ;
Ein neues Opfer fordert er.
  Ein Lamm von aller Makel rein
  Muss deises Bundes Opfer sein.
Den Eingebornen will der Herr ;
Bald kommt—bald fällt—bald blutet er.

The blood of goats the Lord doth will
No more in the new covenant ;
New sacrifice He doth require.
  A Lamb from every blemish pure
  Must of this cov'nant off'ring be.
His only Son the Lord demands ;
He cometh quickly—falls--and bleeds.

A double Chorus now begins, the " Schutzgeister " singing alternately with the People in the Streets of Jerusalem, behind the Scenes.

Chorus. Ich höre schon ein Mordgeschrei !
Volk. Barabbas sei
  Von Banden frei !
Chorus. Nein ! Jesus sei
  Von Banden frei !
Wild tönet, ach ! der Mörder Stimm':
Volk. An's Kreuz mit ihm ! an's Kreuz
  mit ihm !
Chorus. Ach ! seht ihn an ! ach ! seht ihn
  an !
Was hat er böses wohl gethan !
Volk. Entlässt du diesen Bösewicht,
  Dann bist des Kaisers Freund du nicht.

Chorus. A murderous cry e'en now I hear !
People. Barabbas be
  From fetters free !
Chorus. No ! Jesus be
  From fetters free !
Wild rings, alas ! the murderer's cry.
People. To the Cross with Him !
  To the Cross with Him !
Chorus. Behold Him ! ah ! behold ye
  Him !
What evil ever hath He done ?
People. If thou release this wretched One,
  Then art thou not great Cæsar's friend.

Chorus. Jerusalem ! Jerusalem !
  Das Blut des Sohnes rächet noch an euch der Herr.
Volk.   Es falle über uns und unsere Kinder her !
Chorus. Es komme über euch und eure Kinder !

Chorus. Jerusalem ! Jerusalem !
  The blood of His Son will the Lord yet avenge on you !
People. His blood be on us, and on our children !
Chorus. Be it then upon you, and on your children !

SCENE I.

Three bands of the people, each headed by PRIESTS *and* PHARISEES *enter from the three streets of Jerusalem. Traders and Witnesses in each band. The band advancing from the right is led by the priest* NATHANAEL, *that on the left entering by* PILATE'S *house is led by* EZEKIEL. *The middle band is preceded by* CAIAPHAS *and* ANNAS. *Each of the four leaders excites and inflames his band ; even from afar their cry is heard. The four bands advance to the foreground, and unite in one mass, which acts, rages, and cries out as one man. For convenience the four bands of people are denoted by numbers.*

Nathanael. Moses, your prophet, calls upon you ! His holy law calls you to vengeance !

First Band. We belong to Moses ! We are and will remain followers of Moses and of his teaching.

Third Band. We hold fast by our priests and scribes. Away with Him who rises up against them !

Fourth Band. Ye are our fathers. We will answer for your honour.

Annas. Come, children, cast yourselves into the arms of the holy Sanhedrim, it will save you.

Ezekiel. Shake it off, shake it off, the yoke of the Deceiver !

Second Band. We will not know Him any longer, we follow you !

Third Band. The whole people applaud you !

Fourth Band. We will be free from the false Teacher, the Nazarene !

Four Leaders. Your fathers' God will again receive you, ye are once more a holy people unto Him !

The whole Multitude. Ye are our true friends. Long live the great Sanhedrim ! Long live our teachers and priests !

Annas. And death to the Galilæan !

Caiaphas. Up, let us hasten hence to Pilate ! The Nazarene shall die !

The Leaders. He hath falsified the law ! He hath despised Moses and the prophets !

The whole Multitude. Death to the false Prophet !

Second Band. Crucify Him !

Second and Third Bands. Pilate must have Him crucified !

The Leaders. On the cross shall He expiate His crime !

Third and Fourth Bands. We will not rest till the sentence be pronounced. [*The whole crowd of people is now in the foreground.*

Caiaphas (dominating the people with glance and gesture). Hail, children of Israel! Yea, ye are still worthy descendants of your father Abraham! O rejoice that ye have escaped the unspeakable perdition which this Deceiver was fain to bring upon you and your children!

Annas (Caiaphas at his side). Only the untiring efforts of your fathers have preserved the nation from the abyss!

The whole Multitude. Long live the Council! Death to the Nazarene!

Priests and Pharisees. Cursed be he who doth not cry out for His death!

The People. We require His death!

Caiaphas. Let Him be cast out of the heritage of our fathers!

The People. Let him be cast out!

Caiaphas. The Governor will give you the choice between this Blasphemer of God and Barabbas. Let us insist upon the release of Barabbas!

The People. Let Barabbas go free and the Nazarene perish!

Annas. We thank you, O fathers, ye have listened to our desire!

All. Pilate must consent, the whole nation demands it from him!

Caiaphas. Fairest day to the children of Israel! Children, be steadfast!

Priests and Pharisees. This day restores honour to the synagogue and peace to the people.

Caiaphas (approaching PILATE'S *house).* Demand the sentence with tumult. Threaten a universal insurrection!

All (tumultuously). We require the blood of our Enemy!

A Servant of Pilate (rushing out of the house). Uproar! Insurrection!

People. The Nazarene must die!

Caiaphas. Show courage! Stand out unterrified; the righteous cause defends us.

All. Pilate, pronounce the sentence of death!

Servant (from the balcony). Quiet! Peace!

All. No, we will not rest till Pilate consent!

Servant. Pilate will immediately appear. [*Exit.*

All. We demand the death of the Nazarene!

Caiaphas (to the PRIESTS). Now may Pilate, as he desired, be able to learn the mind of the people.

SCENE II. (*See* pp. 26, 27.)

The same. PILATE *with Attendants and with the thorn-crowned* CHRIST, *led by two Soldiers, upon the Balcony.*

All. Give judgment! Sentence Him!

Pilate (pointing to JESUS). Behold the Man!

Priests and Pharisees. Crucify Him!

Pilate. Cannot even this pitiable sight win compassion from your hearts?

All. Let Him die! Crucify Him!

Caiaphas. Hear, O Governor, the voice of the people! it consents to our accusation and demands His death.

People. Yea, we desire His death!

Pilate (to the Soldiers). Lead Him below, and let Barabbas be brought hither from the prison! Let the jailor deliver him up immediately to the chief lictor.

Annas. Let Barabbas live! Pronounce the sentence of death on the Nazarene!

The People. Death to the Nazarene!

Pilate. I cannot comprehend this people. But a few days ago ye followed this Man rejoicing and answering one another with shouts of triumph, through the streets of Jerusalem. Is it possible that to-day the same people should call out for His death and destruction? That is despicable fickleness.

Caiaphas. The good people have at last learnt to see that they were deceived by an Adventurer who pretended to call Himself the Messiah, the King of Israel.

Nathanael. Now the eyes of this people are fully opened, so that they see how that He cannot help Himself,—He, who promised to bring freedom and prosperity to the nation.

Ezekiel. Israel will have no Messiah who lets Himself be taken and bound and treated with every kind of scorn!

The People. Let Him die, the false Messiah, the Deceiver!

Pilate. Men of the Jewish people! ye have a custom that I should release a prisoner unto you at the feast. Look now upon these two! The One—of gentle countenance, of noble demeanour, the Image of a wise Teacher, Whom ye have long honoured as such, convicted of no one evil deed, and already humiliated by the most severe chastisement! the other a vicious, savage man, a convicted robber and murderer, the horrible image of a finished scoundrel! I appeal to your reason, to your human feeling! Choose! Whom will ye that I release unto you, Barabbas, or Jesus, whom ye call Christ?

Priests and People. Let Barabbas go free!

Pilate. Will ye not that I release unto you the King of the Jews?

Priests and People. Away with this Man, and release unto us Barabbas!

Caiaphas. Thou hast promised to release him whom the people should require.

Pilate (to CAIAPHAS). I am accustomed to keep my promise without needing a reminder. (*To the people*) What shall I do, then, with the King of the Jews?

Priests and People. Crucify Him!

Pilate. What, shall I crucify your King?

The People. We have no king but Cæsar.

Pilate. I cannot condemn this Man, for I find no fault in Him. He is sufficiently chastised. I will release Him.

Priest. If thou let this Man go thou art not Cæsar's friend.

Caiaphas. He hath given Himself out as a King.

Priest. And he who pretends to be a king is a rebel against Cæsar.

Nathanaël. And this Rebel is to remain unpunished and to scatter abroad still further the seeds of insurrection?

People. It is the duty of the Governor to put Him out of the way.

Caiaphas. We have done our duty as subjects of Cæsar and deliver this Insurgent to thee. If thou dost not attend to our accusation and the demand of the people, then are we free from guilt. Thou alone, O Governor, art responsible to Cæsar for the consequences!

Annas. If on this Man's account universal tumult and rebellion arise, we shall know who must bear the blame of it, and Cæsar also will know.

People. The matter must be brought before Cæsar.

Ezekiel. With astonishment will it be heard in Rome that Cæsar's Governor protected one guilty of high treason, whose death the entire people demanded.

The People. Thou must cause Him to be condemned, else will there be no peace in the land.

Pilate. What evil hath He done? I cannot and dare not condemn the innocent to death!

Caiaphas. Permit me to ask a question. Wherefore judgest thou this Man so anxiously, when lately thou didst through thy soldiers cause a hundred to be slaughtered without judgment or sentence on account of a rebellious outcry? (PILATE *starts.*)

The People. Thou canst not then show favour to this Man if thou wilt be a true servant of Cæsar.

Pilate. Let water be brought!

Caiaphas. The people will not leave this place until the sentence of death be pronounced upon the Enemy of Cæsar.

The People. Yea, we will not again leave this spot until the sentence is pronounced.

Pilate. Then your violence forces me to comply with your desire. Take Him hence and crucify Him! Yet behold! (*He washes his hands.*)

I wash my hands ; I am innocent of the blood of the Righteous. Ye may answer for it !

Priests and People. We take it upon ourselves. His blood be upon us and upon our children !

Pilate. Let Barabbas, at the demand of the people, be released. Take him away—outside the city gate, so that he never again tread these streets.   [*The Soldiers lead away* BARABBAS.

Priests and People. Now hast thou justly judged !

Pilate. I have yielded to your violent pressure in order to keep off greater evil, but in this blood-guiltiness will I have no part. Let it happen as ye, with tumultuous voices, have called out ; let it be upon you and upon your children !

Priests and People. It is good ; let it be upon us and upon our children !

Annas. We and our children will bless this day, and with thankful joy pronounce the name of Pontius Pilate !

The People. Long live our Governor ! Long live Pontius Pilate !

Pilate. Let the two murderers who are kept in prison be brought here. Let the chief lictor give them over without delay to the soldiers ! They have deserved death—much more than the Accused.

Priests and People. He hath deserved death more than any.

Pilate. The sentence of death must be committed to writing and openly announced before all the people. (*The Scribe begins to write. In the street behind the scenes the soldiers who are bringing in the thieves are heard driving them on : " Will ye get on, ye perverse ones ! Have ye not long ago deserved it ? Thrust them on, the offscouring of mankind ! "*)

Rabbi (pointing to the thieves). There is a worthy companionship for the false Messiah upon His last journey !

Pilate (to the thieves). Of you and of your evil deeds shall the earth this day be quit. Ye shall be crucified.—Let the sentence of death be now read.

Scribe (rises and reads). I, Pontius Pilate, Governor in Judæa of the mighty Emperor Claudius Tiberius, pronounce, at the importunate desire of the high priests of the Sanhedrim, and of the assembled people of the Jews, the sentence of death upon a certain Jesus of Nazareth, Who is accused of having stirred up the people to rebellion, of having forbidden to give tribute to Cæsar, and of having given Himself out as King of the Jews. The same shall outside the city, between two malefactors who for many robberies and murders are likewise condemned to death, be nailed to the cross, and their death thus accomplished. Given at Jerusalem, on the eve of the Passover.

Pilate (breaks his staff). Now take Him hence, and—crucify Him !

                    [*He turns hastily and almost rushes into the house.*

Caiaphas. Triumph ! Victory is ours ! The Enemy of the Synagogue is destroyed !

Priests and People. Away with Him to Golgotha!

The People. Long live the Synagogue!

Priests and Pharisees. Long live the nation!

Annas. Make haste, that we may return home at the right time to eat the Passover lamb!

Priests and Pharisees. With joy shall we keep this feast of the Passover, even as our fathers in Egypt!

Caiaphas. Let our triumphal procession go through the midst of Jerusalem.

Rabbi. Where are His followers? They are invited to cry Hosanna!

The People (going away). Up and away! To Golgotha! Come see Him, how He will die upon the cross! O day of joy, the Enemy of Moses is cast down! So let it be to him who despises the law! He deserves the death of the cross! Auspicious Passover! Now doth joy return to Israel! There is an end of the Galilæan!

[*Exeunt in a tumultuous procession.*

END OF THE SECOND PART.

PART III.

ACT XV.

THE WAY OF THE CROSS. (*See* pp. 27, 28.)

PROLOGUE.

The extorted condemnation has been pronounced. Now we see Jesus fainting on the way to the Mount of Golgotha, laden with the beam of the Cross. Isaac also once bore willingly upon his own shoulders the wood for the offering to the mountain where he was to bleed as a sacrifice according to the word of Jehovah. Jesus also bears willingly the wood of the Cross, which through the offering of holy love will now soon become a Tree of Life rich in blessing. For as a glance at the brazen serpent set up in the wilderness brought healing, so comfort and blessing come to us from the Tree of the Cross.

Chorus.

Betet an und habet Dank !	Pray, and render heartfelt thanks !
Der den Kelch der Leiden trank,	He who drank the cup of pain
Geht nun in den Kreuzestod	To the cross of death now goes,
Und versöhnt die Welt mit Gott.	Reconciles the world with God.

FIRST TABLEAU. —ISAAC BEARING THE WOOD UP MOUNT MORIAH.

Chorus.

Wie das Opferholz getragen	E'en as the wood for sacrifice
Isaak selbst auf Moria,	Isaac himself to Moriah bore,
Wanket, mit dem Kreuz beladen,	With His Cross laden, Jesus faints,
Jesus hin nach Golgatha.	Yet bears it on to Golgotha.
Betet an und habet Dank, &c.	Pray, and render heartfelt thanks, &c.

SECOND TABLEAU.—THE BRAZEN SERPENT.

Chorus.

Angenagelt wird erhöhet	Nailed, and raised upon the Cross
An dem Kreuz der Menschensohn.	Soon will be the Son of man.
Hier an Moses Schlange sehet,	Here in Moses' serpent see
Ihr des Kreuzes Vorbild schon.	Type already of the Cross.
Betet an und habet Dank, &c.	Pray, and render heartfelt thanks, &c.

THIRD TABLEAU.—THE CHILDREN OF ISRAEL AROUND THE BRAZEN
SERPENT.

Chorus.

Von den gift'gen Schlangenbissen
  Ward dadurch das Volk befreit !
So wird von dem Kreuze fliessen
  Auf uns Heil und Seligkeit.
    Betet an und habet Dank, &c.
	From the pois'nous serpents' bite
	Were the people healed through this !
	So will from the Cross to us
	Healing flow and blessedness.
	    Pray, and render heartfelt thanks, &c.

SCENE I.

The Holy Women with JOHN *and* JOSEPH *of Arimathea coming from
Bethany.*

Mary (*to* JOHN). O beloved disciple, how has it gone with my
Jesus ?

John. If the priests could do as they willed, so were He surely already
amongst the dead, but they dare not carry out the sentence without per-
mission of the Governor, and Pilate, I hope, will not condemn Him, since
He hath ever only done good.

Magdalene. The Lord guide the heart of the Governor !

Mary. O friends, whither shall we go, that I may again see my Son ?

Joseph. There is no one to be seen from whom we could obtain
tidings.

John. It will be best to go to Nicodemus, who surely knows how it
is with the Master.

Mary. Yea, let us go thither. Every moment increases my anguish.

John. Be strong in faith, beloved Mother. (*Cries are heard, " On, on
with Him ! " It is the people, urging on* JESUS, *who has fallen under His
burden.*)

Joseph. What fearful tumult is that ?   [*They stand still, listening.*

SCENE II.

The Procession of the Cross-bearing, PRIESTS, PHARISEES, *People, Soldiers, half in the " Street of Annas," turning slowly into the foreground. In front the Centurion with the staff of command, a
horseman in the group with the Roman banner.* CHRIST *painfully
dragging the Cross, nearest to Him the four Executioners.*

People. Let Him die, and all who hold with Him !

First Executioner. Is the burden already too heavy for Thee ?

People. Urge Him on with force that we may get to Calvary !

Second Executioner. Hold hard, He will come down again !

[*The group in the " Street of Pilate " know not yet what is going on.*

Joseph. What shall we do ? With this crowd we cannot venture our-selves in the city.

Mary. What may this tumult signify ? Can it possibly concern my Son ?

Joseph. It seems as if an insurrection had broken out.

John. We will keep quiet here until the storm has blown over.

Simon of Cyrene (comes hastily and anxiously from the middle street to the foreground carrying a basket). I must hasten in order to get into the city. The eve of the feast is on the decline, and I must yet make purchases.

Priests and People (still unseen by SIMON). Let Him not rest! Urge Him on with blows!

Simon. What an outcry! I will keep myself quiet.

Third Executioner. Thy fainting avails Thee nothing, Thou must get out to Golgotha.

Ahasuerus (coming quickly out of his house). Away from my house! This is no place for repose.

Simon. The tumult becomes greater.—Who comes there ? I will await the event.

SCENE III.

The Procession with CHRIST *has at last come to the front. Meanwhile from the Middle Street* VERONICA *and the Women of Jerusalem draw near.*

John. It seems that some one is led out to execution at Calvary.

Mary (sees JESUS). It is He! O God, it is my Son! (*Those around* JESUS *push Him on.*)

Executioner. He delays us on the road.

Centurion (to JESUS, *who in uttermost weariness has again fallen fainting*). Here, refresh Thyself! (*He hands Him a flask,* JESUS *takes it but does not drink.*)

Mary. Ah, see Him thus led to death, like to a malefactor, between two malefactors!

John. Mother, it is the hour of which He spoke before ; thus it is the Father's will.

Centurion. Wilt Thou not drink ? Then force Him on.

Fourth Executioner (shakes JESUS). Bestir Thyself, lazy King of the Jews!

Second Executioner. Up, pull Thyself together!

Third Executioner. Do not act so weakly, we must get on.

Mary. O, where is any sorrow like unto my sorrow!

Third Executioner. He is too much exhausted ; some one must help, otherwise——

Rabbi (pointing out SIMON). Here, this stranger——

I

Pharisee. Lay hold on him !

Centurion. Come hither, thou hast broad shoulders.

Simon. I must——

Fourth Executioner. Indeed thou must, or there will be blows.

Pharisee. Beat him if he will not go.

Simon. I am indeed innocent, I have committed no crime.

Executioner. Silence !

Simon (*observing* CHRIST). What do I see ? that is the Holy Man of Nazareth !

Second Executioner. Thy shoulders here !

Simon. For love of Thee will I bear it. O that I could thereby make myself worthy in Thy sight !

Christ (*standing exhausted at one side*). God's blessing upon thee and thine.

Executioner. Forward now, do Thou follow after with the beam of the Cross !

First Priest (*to* CHRIST). Now canst Thou step on quickly.

Third Executioner (*seizing* JESUS *by the neck and shaking Him*). See how we are kept back by Thee, even though the instrument of punishment be taken off Thee !

Second Executioner. Dost Thou need anything more ?

Executioner. Let Him alone, we will wait a little longer yet that He may revive before we go up the hill.

[VERONICA *and the Women of Jerusalem approach the procession.*

Caiaphas. Another stoppage already ? When shall we get to Calvary ?

Veronica (*kneeling before* JESUS *and offering Him a napkin*). O Lord, how is Thy countenance covered with blood and sweat ! Wilt Thou not wipe it ?

Christ (*wipes His face and gives her back the cloth*). Compassionate soul, the Father will recompense thee for it.

Women of Jerusalem (*kneeling with their little ones before the* LORD). Thou good Master, never-to-be-forgotten Benefactor, noblest Friend of men, thus art Thou recompensed ! (*They weep.*)

Christ. Daughters of Jerusalem, weep not for me, but weep for yourselves and for your children. For behold, the days are coming in the which they shall say, Blessed are the barren, and the wombs that never bare, and the paps that never gave suck. Then shall they begin to say to the mountains, Fall on us ; and to the hills, Cover us. For if they do these things in a green tree, what shall be done in the dry ?

Centurion. Now remove the women folk.

Third Executioner. What good are your women's tears ? Back !

Second and Fourth Executioners. Away with Him to the hill of death !

People. Up briskly to Calvary !

Rabbi. Is the thing ever to go on?

Nathanael. The Centurion is quite too merciful.

Priest. He does not spare his soldiers so much.

[*The procession begins to move forward; the Servant of* PILATE *appears.*

SCENE IV.

Pilate's Servant. Hold! By the Governor's command, the Centurion is immediately to appear before him and to receive further directions.

[*The procession stops.*

Caiaphas. What is this? Wherefore any new directions? The sentence of death is pronounced and must be carried out without delay.

Centurion (sternly). No, this cannot be, until I shall have received the orders of my lord. (*To the Soldiers*) Keep ye watch meanwhile, and go on with the condemned towards Golgotha. Then dismiss this man (*pointing to* SIMON) and await my arrival.

[*Exit with the Servant. The procession moves forward again towards the middle of the background.*

People (wildly, one to another). Up to Golgotha! Crucify Him! Hail to Israel, the Enemy is overcome! We are set free, long live the Sanhedrim!

John. Mother, shall we not return to Bethany? Thou wilt not be able to bear the sight.

Mary. How could a mother leave her child in the last bitterest need! I will suffer with Him, with Him bear scorn and shame—die with Him!

John. If only strength of body do not fail.

Mary. Fear not. I have prayed to God for strength, the Lord hath heard me. Let us follow after.

All. Dearest Mother, we follow thee. (*They slowly follow the procession.*)

ACT XVI.

JESUS ON CALVARY.

PROLOGUE.

Chorus (clothed in black).

Auf, fromme Seelen, auf und gehet	Up, pious souls, arise and go
Von Reue, Schmerz und Dank durchglüht,	Full of remorse, of pain, and thanks,
Mit mir zu Golgatha, und sehet,	With me to Golgotha, and see
Was hier zu eurem Heil geschieht.	What for your saving here befell.
Dort stirbt der Mittler zwischen Gott	There dies the Daysman between God
Und Sünder den Vermittlungstod.	And sinners, the atoning death.

Ach ! nackt, von Wunden nur bekleidet,
Liegt er hier bald am Kreuz für dich ;
Die Rache der Gottlosen weidet
An seiner Blösse frevelnd sich,
　　Und er, der dich, o Sünder, liebt,—
　　Schweigt, leidet, duldet und vergibt.

Ah ! naked, only cloth'd with wounds,
Here lies He on the Cross for thee ;
The vengeance of the wicked gloats,
Malicious, o'er His nakedness,
　　And He, who thee, O sinner, loves,
　　Is silent, suffers, and forgives.

Ich hör' schon seine Glieder krachen,
Die man aus den Gelenken zerrt,
Wem soll's das Herz nicht beben machen,
Wenn er den Streich des Hammers hört,
　　Der schmetternd, ach ! durch Hand
　　　　und Fuss,
　　Grausame Nägel treiben muss.

I hear His limbs already crack,
As they from out their joints are dragg'd ;
Whose heart doth it not cause to quake
When he the hammer's stroke doth hear,
　　Whose ringing blows, through hands and
　　　　feet,
　　Alas ! the cruel nails must drive ?

The blows of the hammer are heard behind the scenes.   The curtain rises ; CHRIST
lies upon the Cross.

Choragus (intones, accompanied by soft music).

Auf, fromme Seelen ! naht dem Lamme
Das sich für euch freiwillig schenkt
Betrachtet es am Kreuzes stamme :
Seht, zwischen Mörder aufgehängt
Gibt Gottes Sohn sein Blut, und ihr
Gebt keine Thräne ihm dafür ?

Up, pious souls, draw near the Lamb
Who freely gives Himself for you.
Behold Him on the Tree of doom,
See how He hangs 'twixt murderers,
He, Son of God, His life-blood gives,
And ye no tears give back to Him ?

Selbst seinen Mördern zu vergeben,
Hört man ihn gleich zum Vater fleh'n,
Und bald, bald endigt er sein Leben,
Damit wir ew'gem Tod entgeh'n.
　　Durch seine Seite dringt ein Speer
　　Und öffnet uns sein Herz noch mehr.

Himself His murderers to forgive,
We hear Him to the Father pray ;
And soon, O soon, He ends His life,
That we eternal death may 'scape.
His side a spear doth pierce full sore,
And opes to us His heart still more.

Choragus (sings).

Wer kann die hohe Liebe fassen,
　　Die bis zum Tode liebt,
Und statt der Mörder Schaar zu hassen,
　　Noch segnend ihr vergibt.

O who can this high love conceive
Which loveth even unto death,
And blessing e'en the murd'rous band,
Instead of hating, pardons them ?

The whole Chorus.

O bringet dieser Liebe
Nur fromme Herzenstriebe
　　Am Kreuzaltar
　　Zum Opfer dar.

O bring to this great Love
But pious heart's emotion,
Upon the Altar of the Cross
To the great Offering there.

SCENE I. (*See pp. 28, 29.*)

　　The scene is in the middle of the stage. As the curtain rises, the two crosses with the malefactors are raised. Christ lies, nailed to His Cross, on the ground. Lictors, executioners, high priests, Pharisees, people ; in the background the Holy Women, with John, Joseph, and Nicodemus.

The Executioners (pointing to the thieves). We have already finished with these. Now must the King of the Jews be also raised on high upon His throne.

Priest. Not King!—Deceiver! Chief traitor!

Centurion. First, however, this writing must, according to the Governor's order, be fastened to the Cross. Faustus! fasten this escutcheon over the Cross.

Faustus. A shield exposed to public view! Ha, that is truly regal! (*He fastens on the writing.*)

Centurion. Now lay hold, and raise the Cross! only not carelessly!

Third Executioner. Come, redouble your efforts! (*They raise it.*)

Fourth Executioner. All right, the Cross stands firm!

Centurion. The painful act is accomplished.

Caiaphas. And truly admirably accomplished. Thanks and applause from us all.

Pharisee. Thanks and applause from us all.

Caiaphas. This day shall be for ever a feast day.

Pharisee. Yea, it will be solemnly kept for all time to come.

Annas. And I will now willingly go down to my fathers since I have lived to have the joy of seeing this wretch upon the Cross. But the writing upon the Cross seems to me to be very briefly composed.

Rabbi (going closer). That is an affront to the Sanhedrim and to the people!

Caiaphas. What is written?

Rabbi. It reads thus: Jesus of Nazareth, the King of the Jews! (*The four Executioners lie down under the Cross.*)

Caiaphas (reads). Truly the honour of the nation is therein touched.

Priest. Let the writing be torn down.

Caiaphas. We dare not ourselves lay hands on it. (*To two Priests*) Go to the Governor and demand, in the name of the Sanhedrim and of the assembled people, the alteration of this writing. He should write that He *said*—I am the King of the Jews. Then also present a petition that before the great eve of the feast the bones of the crucified be broken and their bodies taken down. [*Exit the two Priests.*

Third Executioner. Now, comrades, let us divide what has fallen to us. (*He takes up the coat and the mantle of* CHRIST.) See, the mantle makes just four parts. (*The four Executioners seize the mantle and tear it, with one pull, into four pieces.*) But the coat is not sewn together. Shall we cut it also in pieces?

Second Executioner. No, it is better that we cast lots for it.

First Executioner. Here are dice. I will at once try my luck. (*He throws.*) That is too little. I have lost.

Third Executioner (looking up to CHRIST). What? If thou canst work a miracle upon the Cross then give luck to my throw. (*He throws.*)

The other Executioners. What does He know about us?

Fourth Executioner. I ought to be luckier. Fifteen! Very good. Now do thou try it!

Second Executioner. I must get it. (*He throws.*)

Third Executioner (*looking at the dice*). Eighteen! That is the highest.

First Executioner. It is thine, take it away.

Fourth Executioner. Thou art not at all to be envied about it.

Rabbi (*returning from* PILATE). Our embassy was fruitless. He would not listen to us.

Caiaphas. Did he give you no answer?

Rabbi. This only: "What I have written I have written."

Annas (*aside*). Intolerable!

Caiaphas. What answer did he give you concerning breaking the bones?

Rabbi. Concerning that, he said he would give his orders to the Centurion.

Priest (*to* CHRIST). Therefore the writing remains: King of the Jews. Ah, if Thou art a King in Israel come down now from the Cross that we may see it and believe on Thee.

Second Priest. Thou that destroyest the Temple and buildest it in three days, save Thyself!

Caiaphas. Ah, Thou hast saved others, Thyself thou canst not save.

The False Witnesses. Come down, for Thou art the Son of God!

Annas. He trusted in God: let Him deliver Him now if He will have Him.

Fourth Executioner. What! dost Thou not hear?

First and Third Executioners. Show Thy power, mighty King of the Jews!

Christ (*whose head during the whole time has hung motionless, now turns it painfully*). Father, forgive them, for they know not what they do!

The Thief on the left (*to* CHRIST). Hearest Thou? If Thou art the Christ, save Thyself and us.

The Thief on the right (*to him on the left*). Dost thou not fear God, seeing thou art in the same condemnation? And we indeed justly; for we receive the due reward of our deeds; but this Man hath done nothing amiss. Lord, remember me when Thou comest into Thy kingdom.

Christ. Verily I say unto thee, To-day shalt thou be with me in paradise.   [MARY *and* JOHN *draw near to the Cross.*

Caiaphas. Listen, He still goes on as though it were His to command at the doors of paradise!

Rabbi. His presumption has not yet left Him, now that He hangs helpless upon the Cross!

Christ. Woman, behold thy son! Son, behold thy Mother!

Mary. Thus dying Thou carest still for Thy Mother!

John. Sacred to me be thy last will! Thou my Mother! And I thy son!

Christ (with signs of the approaching end). I thirst.

Centurion. He suffers thirst and asks for drink.

Second Executioner. I will quickly reach it to Him (*he takes the reed with the sponge, upon which the Centurion pours from his flask;* CHRIST *sips from the sponge*). Here, drink!

Christ (with the expression of deepest anguish). Eloi, Eloi, lama sabachthani ?

Pharisee and People. See, He calleth Elias!

Caiaphas. Let be, let us see whether Elias will come to save Him.

Christ (breathing heavily several times). It is finished! Father, into Thy hands I commend my spirit. (*He slowly droops His head and dies. Thunder is heard ; it becomes dark.*)

Priests and People. What a fearful earthquake! Hear ye the crash of the falling rocks? Woe to us!

Centurion. Certainly this was a righteous Man!

Soldiers. The Godhead Himself bears Him witness through these terrors of nature!

Centurion. This patience in fiercest pains, this noble calm, this loud devout cry to Heaven in the moment before His departure—all makes one augurate something higher. Truly He is the Son of God!

People. Come, neighbours, I will remain no longer in this place of horrors. Let us return home. God be gracious to us!

Others (smiting on their breasts). Almighty One! we have sinned! (*The people disperse with signs of sorrow and remorse.*)

Servant of the Temple (enters hastily). High Priests and assembled Council! In the holy place a fearful event has happened! I tremble in every limb.

Caiaphas. What is it? not the Temple——

Annas. Thrown down?

Servant. Not that, but the veil of the Temple is rent in twain from the top to the bottom. It seemed as though the whole earth were split asunder.

Priests and Pharisees. Terrible!·

Caiaphas (pointing to the dead JESUS*).* This has that wretch done for us through His enchantments! It is well that He is out of the world, else would He bring all the elements into disorder.

Priests and Pharisees. Curse upon Him, who is in league with Beelzebub !

Caiaphas. Let us go home with haste and see what has happened ; then will we immediately return hither again. For I have no rest until I have seen that the legs of this Man be broken, and His Body thrown into the malefactor's grave! [*Exeunt the* PRIESTS.

Scene II.

Nicodemus (to Joseph *of Arimathea).* Shall then the holy Body of the God-sent be so fearfully dishonoured as to be thrown into the malefactor's grave ?

Joseph. Friend, hear my resolve. I will go straightway to Pilate and will earnestly beg of him that he will give me the Body of Jesus. This favour he will not deny me.

Nicodemus. Do so, friend ! I will bring spices to embalm Him.

[*Exeunt.*

Centurion (to the Holy Women). Fear ye not, good women. No evil shall befall you.

Magdalene (clasping the Cross). O most beloved Teacher, my heart hangs with Thee upon the Cross !

Servant of Pilate *(entering, to the* Centurion*).* By order of my lord, the crucified are to have their legs broken. And then their bodies are to be taken down. Before the beginning of the great eve all must be over.

Centurion. It will be done at once. Fellows, break first the bones of these two.

Third Executioner. Let us bring this heart-breaking business quickly to an end.

Second Executioner (who has gone up a ladder to the Thief on the right hand, and with four blows of a club broken his legs). He wakes no more !

Fourth Executioner (goes up to the Thief on the left hand). The other will I hasten out of the world.

Mary (shuddering). Ah, Jesus, they will not surely deal so horribly with Thy holy Body ?

Fourth Executioner (to the Thief on the left hand). Movest thou not any more ? No ; he has his wages !

Magdalene (as the Executioner with a club goes towards Christ*).* Ah, spare Him ! spare Him !

Third Executioner (looking up to Christ*).* He is already deceased. Breaking His legs is no longer necessary.

Second Executioner. In order that we may be quite sure of His death I will open His heart with a spear. (*He pierces* Jesus *in the side ; the blood flows out.*

The Holy Women. Ah !

Magdalene. O Mother ! This wound has also pierced thy heart !

Centurion. Now take the Body from the Cross !

First Executioner. Whither then with it ?

Centurion. As it is ordered—into the criminal's grave.

Mary. What a fearful word !

Fourth Executioner. Ladders here ! They will soon be taken down !

Magdalene (to the Centurion*).* May we not then once show the last honours to our Friend ?

Centurion. Unhappily it lies not in my power to fulfil your wish.

Second Executioner (to the First, who stands upon the ladder). Go thou up, I will hold.

Third Executioner. And I will look after the others. (*He mounts the ladder.*)

SCENE III. (*See* p. 30.)

The PRIESTS *return to Golgotha.*

Caiaphas (entering at the head of the PRIESTS*).* It will be the more grateful to us to see the Body of the wretch thrown into the grave of shame, that we have beheld the destruction which He has brought to pass in the Temple.

Annas. It would rejoice mine eyes to see His limbs torn asunder by wild beasts!

Caiaphas. See, they have been already taken down. So we shall see our wish fulfilled at once.

Pilate's Servant (entering with JOSEPH *of Arimathea, to the* CENTURION*).* The Governor hath sent me to inquire of thee whether Jesus of Nazareth be indeed dead already, as this man here hath told him.

Centurion. It is so; see for thyself.

Servant. Then I am commissioned to announce to thee that His Body is to be delivered over to this man as a gift from the Governor.   [*Exit.*

The Holy Women. O comfortable tidings!

Rabbi (looking towards JOSEPH *of Arimathea).* The betrayer of the Synagogue! So he has again worked secretly!

Annas. And destroyed our joy!

Caiaphas (to the CENTURION*).* Nevertheless, we will not consent that He be laid in any other place than with the malefactors.

Centurion. Since the Body is given to this man it goes without saying that he can bury it how and where he wishes. This allows of no objection. (*To the Soldiers and Executioners*) Men! our business is ended, we will return home.   [*Exit.*

Annas (to JOSEPH *of Arimathea).* Thou persistest, then, in thy stubbornness? Art thou not ashamed to honour, even in His corpse, a condemned Criminal?

Joseph. I honour the most virtuous of Men, the God-sent Teacher, the innocent, murdered One!

Nicodemus. Envy and pride were the motives of His condemnation. The judge himself was forced to testify to His innocence; he swore that he would have no part in His blood.

Caiaphas. The curse of the law will bring you to destruction, ye enemies of our fathers!

Rabbi. Do not excite thyself, High Priest, they are smitten with blindness !

Caiaphas. Cursed be ye by the whole Council ! Bereft of your dignities, never more shall ye dare to appear in our midst !

Nicodemus. We also desire never more to do so.

Annas (*coming forward with the* PRIESTS). As the Body is in the hands of His friends we must be on our guard, since this Deceiver said in His lifetime that after three days He would rise again.

Rabbi. How easily could a new trick be played upon the people, and fresh embarrassment be prepared for us ! His disciples could take Him away secretly and then spread abroad the saying that He had risen.

Caiaphas. Then were the last error worse than the first. Let us then go immediately to Pilate and ask from him a guard of soldiers so that the grave may be watched until the third day.

Annas. A prudent thought !

Rabbi. Thus will their plans be brought to nothing.

[*Exeunt the* PRIESTS.

SCENE IV.

The taking down from the Cross and the Burial.

Magdalene. At length they have gone, the madmen ! Be comforted, beloved Mother ! The mocking and the blasphemy are over, and a holy evening calm surrounds us.

Mary. He has finished it; He has departed into the rest of the Father.

Magdalene. He has not been torn from us for ever, that is His own promise.

Mary (*to the men busied about the taking down from the Cross*). Generous men ! Bring quickly to me the Body of my beloved Child !

Salome. Come, my companions, prepare this winding-sheet to receive it. (*They place* MARY *upon a stone and spread out the winding-sheet at her feet.*)

Joseph (*taking the Body of* JESUS *upon his shoulders*). O sweet, O holy burden, rest upon my shoulders ! (*He lifts the Body down.*)

Nicodemus (*stretching out his arms to receive the Body*). Come, holy Body of my only Friend ! Let me embrace Thee ! How hath the fury of Thy enemies lacerated Thee ! (*The Body is placed leaning on* MARY'S *breast.*)

John. Here shall the Best of sons rest once more in the bosom of the Best of mothers.

Mary. O my Son, how is Thy Body covered with wounds !

John. Mother, from these wounds flow healing and blessing for mankind.

Magdalene. Behold, Mother, heaven's peace rests upon the dead countenance !

Nicodemus. Let us anoint Him and wrap Him in this new winding-sheet.

Joseph. He shall be laid in my new grave which I have prepared for myself in the rocky cave in my garden.

Salome. Best of Masters ! One more loving tear upon Thy lifeless Body !

Magdalene. O let me kiss once more the hand which so often blessed me !

John. We shall see Him again !

Joseph (*to* NICODEMUS). Do thou help me to bear Him into the garden.

Nicodemus. I am blessed, since I may lay to rest the remains of Him who was sent from God. (*They bear the Body to the grave.*)

John. Let us follow.

Mary. It is the last service which I can do to my Jesus. (*They all follow. The grave is seen in the background.*)

All. Friend, rest softly in the still grave hewn out in the rock !

John. Now will we return home. Come, dearest Mother !

[*Exit with the Women.*

Joseph. Let us close up the grave with this stone ; help me.

Nicodemus. After the feast day we will finish the work of love.

Joseph. Come now, O friend, to lament His death.

Nicodemus. O how can this Man, full of grace and truth, have deserved such a fate ! [*Exeunt.*

ACT XVII.

THE RESURRECTION.

PROLOGUE. (*See* p. 31.)

All is now accomplished. Peace and joy ! His strife hath brought us freedom, His death hath brought us life. O, let the heart of the redeemed glow with thankfulness and love ! The holy One rests in the tomb. Yet for shortest rest. For the Anointed One cannot see corruption ; alive again He will arise. Jonas, God's prophet, after three days came out of the fish's belly. Israel went victoriously through the waves of the sea, which swallowed up the enemy that followed. So will the Lord mightily burst the gates of death, shining out of darkness in glorious light, and arise, to the confusion of His enemies, in exceeding majesty.

Chorus.

Liebe ! Liebe ! In dem Blute	Love ! O Love ! in Thy dear blood
Kämpftest Du mit Gottes Muthe	Thou didst strive with God's own pow'r
Deinen grossen Kampf hinaus.	All Thy mighty combat through.
Liebe ! Du gabst selbst das Leben	Love ! Thou gav'st Thyself Thy life
Für uns Sünder willig hin :	For us sinners willingly :
Stets soll uns vor Augen schweben	Ever 'fore our eyes shall float
Deiner Liebe hoher Sinn.	Higher sense of all Thy love.
Ruhe sanft nun, heil'ge Hülle,	Softly now, O Sacred Frame,
In des Felsengrabes Stille	Rest in stillness of the grave,
Von den heissen Leiden aus !	All Thy bitter passion o'er !
Ruhe sanft im Schooss der Erde,	In earth's lap, O softly rest
Bis Du wirst verkläret sein.	Till Thy glory be reveal'd.
Der Verwesung Moder werde	Never shall corruption's worm
Nie Dein heiliges Gebein.	Touch or mar Thy holy Flesh.

FIRST TABLEAU.—JONAH CAST BY THE WHALE UPON DRY LAND.

Wie Jonas in des Fisches Bauche—	As Jonah once within the fish
So ruhet in der Erde Schooss	So in earth's bosom now doth rest
Des Menschen Sohn—Mit einem Hauche	The Son of man.—But with one breath
Reisst Bande er und Siegel los.	He breaks His bonds and the seal'd tomb.
Triumph ! Triumph ! Er wird ersteh'n.	Victory ! vict'ry ! He will rise.
Wie Jonas aus des Fisches Bauch,	As Jonah from the fish's maw,
So wird der Sohn des Menschen auch	So also will the Son of man
Neu lebend aus dem Grabe geh'n.	Go forth to life from out the grave.

SECOND TABLEAU.—THE EGYPTIANS DROWNED IN THE RED SEA.

Chorus.

Gross ist der Herr ! Gross seine Güte !	Great is the Lord ! His goodness great
Er nahm sich seines Volkes an.	Accepted hath He now His own.
Er führte durch der Wogen Mitte	He led once through the waters' midst
Einst Israel auf trockner Bahn.	His Israel on the firm dry ground.
Triumph, der todt war, wird ersteh'n ;	Triumph, for He who died will rise ;
Ihn decket nicht des Todes Nacht.	Death darkness covers Him no more,
Neu lebend wird aus eigner Macht	New living, He through His own might
Der Sieger aus dem Grabe geh'n.	Will Victor from the grave go forth.

SCENE I.

The Watch sitting or lying about the Grave.

Watch (one after another). Brother, how goes it with thee ? I shall soon find it too wearisome to guard a dead body.—This tedious office of watching the dead, which the priests have put upon us !—Have patience, it is the last night.—But it is truly laughable how this people still fear even the dead.—The Man out of Nazareth must have said that He would rise again on the third day. Hence their anxiety !—If He is really a higher Being, who will then hinder His resurrection? Certainly we cannot!—Who could withstand the will of God, if He willed to permit any one to return from the under world? They fear that His disciples will take away the Body, and that then they can say that He is risen; to prevent this are we set to watch.—Then they may be without anxiety. They are not thinking of it. That would give us a fine hare-hunt! We have been told how bravely they behaved in the olive garden.—The glow of morning is beginning already. (*Earthquake.*) What a fearful earthquake! Ye gods! Away from the rock, it totters, it falls in! (*An Angel rolls away the stone.* CHRIST *arises.*) Immortal gods, what do I see! I am blinded! (*They fall to the ground.*) The appearance is gone!—I saw at the grave a Figure like that of a man, but His face was dazzling as the lightning. Higher powers are at work here.—The grave is open! I see no corpse. He must be risen! He has fulfilled His word. We will hasten to the high priests and relate the whole occurrence to them.

SCENE II.

The Holy Women at the Grave.

Magdalene (hastening on before the others). How does my heart rejoice to show even this honour to the Beloved!

The other Women. Who shall roll us away the stone?

Magdalene (comes from the grave). O sisters, what have I seen! They have taken away the Lord out of the sepulchre!

Women. O God!

Magdalene. I will go at once to Peter and John and bring them these sorrowful tidings. [*Exit.*

Women. Alas, the last consolation is thus taken from us!—Perchance Joseph hath laid Him in another grave.—If only the enemies have not stolen Him away.—Let us see ourselves. (*They go to the grave.*) I see not the Sacred Body. O, I am affrighted!

Angel (appearing at the door of the sepulchre). Fear not! Ye seek Jesus of Nazareth, who was crucified. He is risen, and is no longer here. Go and tell His disciples and Peter that the Lord goeth before you into Galilee. There shall ye see Him as He said unto you. [*Exit.*

Women (departing hastily in terror, then recollecting themselves). What a heavenly message! He is risen! Let us hasten and bring the tidings to all the disciples which the Angel hath brought to us. [*Exeunt.*

SCENE III.

The PRIESTS and the Watch.

Caiaphas. It cannot possibly have happened as the watch declared. (*He goes quickly to the grave.*) It is true! The stone is rolled away, the sepulchre is empty! (*To the Watch*) How did this happen? Confess, or the most fearful punishment awaits you!

Watch. We can say nothing different from what we have already reported.

Pharisees. Ye lie!

Watch. But how could any one have entered, when the door was closed and we sat around the sepulchre?

Caiaphas. Ye are yourselves in the plot.

Annas. Why did ye not at once raise an alarm?

. *Watch.* When a thunderbolt had stricken us to earth!

Rabbi. Whither was the Body taken away?

Watch. That we know not. He is risen, as ye feared. We are going to Pilate, who shall decide, and in the whole city will we make known what we have seen.

Caiaphas (*whispers to the* PRIESTS). We must keep them back. (*To the Watch*) Believe what ye will. Meanwhile, it is our duty to see that the event remain in obscurity. Your silence shall bring you a rich reward.

Watch. But the thing will become known, and for such a deception Pilate would punish us severely.

Annas. For that leave us to take thought.

Caiaphas (*gives money to the Watch*). We will answer for you to Pilate.

Watch (*taking the money*). But if we are questioned?

Caiaphas. Then say ye only: His disciples came while we slept and stole Him away.

Watch. Then take back your money! For such words Pilate would the most severely punish us.

Caiaphas. I will answer for it to you, in the name of the whole Council, that ye shall come off unpunished.

Pharisee. Be without anxiety and be silent.

Watch. We will be silent!   [*Exeunt.*

Caiaphas (*to his followers*). Now seize every opportunity to spread abroad among the people that the Body was taken away by His followers. The victory is ours, the Enemy is dead. His Body may lie where it will! In a few years will the name of the Nazarene be forgotten, or only named with scorn. His work is at an end.   [*Exeunt.*

SCENE IV.

JOHN, PETER, MAGDALENE, *then* CHRIST *and an* ANGEL.

John. I will convince myself whether Mary saw rightly. (*He looks into the sepulchre.*) It is empty! But to enter it I dare not.

Peter. We must, however, search more closely (*coming out of the grave*). Behold thyself, John, how orderly the napkins are folded together by themselves. All is arranged in the grave as when one who arises from sleep lays his night-garments in the appointed place.

John. O Simon, what thoughts do thy words awaken in me! Is the Lord perchance arisen from death as from a gentle sleep?

Peter. If that were true! But I never took that prophecy to the letter.

John. I doubt no longer!

Peter. God grant it! We will now hasten to our brethren and bring them this consolation. Mary, comest thou not with us?

Magdalene. Let me weep here alone!

John. Do not linger too long, Mary!   [*Exit with* PETER.

Magdalene. Now flow down, O tears!

Angel (*appearing at the sepulchre*). Woman, why weepest thou?

Magdalene. Alas, they have taken away my Lord, and I know not where they have laid Him.

Christ (*appearing amongst the trees*). Woman, why weepest thou?

Magdalene. Sir, if Thou have borne Him hence, tell me where Thou hast laid Him.

Christ. Mary!

Magdalene. O, that is His voice! Rabboni!

Christ. Touch me not, for I am not yet ascended to my Father. But go to my brethren, and say unto them: I ascend unto my Father and your Father, and to my God and your God! (*He disappears.*)

Magdalene. O my Master! He hath vanished. But I have seen Him—have heard the beloved voice! Now depart hence, sorrow and sadness! I will hasten as upon wings to the brethren, and will announce to them the greeting of the risen One! O that I could proclaim it throughout all worlds, that mountains and floods, heaven and earth, might re-echo: Hallelujah, He is risen!

THE LAST SCENE. (*See* p. 31.)

PROLOGUE.

He is risen! Rejoice, ye heavens! He is risen! Rejoice, ye mortals! The Lion of the tribe of Judah! He hath bruised the serpent's head. Faith stands firm! The fore-image and pledge of our future resurrection awakes joyful hope in our heart. Cry with the voice of rejoicing, Hallelujah! We saw Him enter Jerusalem in humility, and, ah! for the deepest humiliation. Now let us behold, before we separate, the victorious solemnity of the Conqueror! Now He ascends to the highest glory, full of majesty, to the New Jerusalem, where He will gather to

Himself all whom He hath purchased with His blood. Strengthened and full of joy at this sight, return to your homes, O friends, filled with inmost love for Him Who loved you even unto death, and still in heaven everlastingly loves you—there, where the eternal song of triumph resounds : Praise be to the Lamb which was slain! There, reunited around our Saviour, we shall all meet again! Hallelujah!

Chorus.

Halleluja !	Hallelujah !
Ueberwunden, überwunden	The Hero hath conquered
Hat der Held der Feinde Macht.	The might of the foe !
Er—er schlummerte nur Stunden	Few hours in the grave—
In der düstern Grabesnacht.	In the gloom hath He slept !
Singet Ihm in heil'gen Psalmen !	Sing to Him in holy Psalms !
Streuet Ihm des Sieges Palmen !	Strew before Him Conqu'ror's palms !
Auferstanden ist der Herr !	The Lord He hath risen !
Jauchzet Ihm, ihr Himmel zu !	Rejoice, O ye Heavens !
Sing' dem Sieger, Erde du !	Sing, Earth, to the Victor !
Halleluja Dir Erstandner !	To Thee Who hast risen
	Hallelujah !

LAST TABLEAU.—CHRIST IN GLORY ; HIS ENEMIES UNDER HIS FEET.

Chorus.

Preis Ihm, dem Todes überwinder	Praise Him, Conqueror of Death,
Der einst verdammt auf Gabbatha !	Once condemned on Gabbatha !
Preis Ihm dem Heiliger der Sünder,	Praise Him, amidst sinners Holy,
Der für uns starb auf Golgatha !	Who for us on Calvary died !
Bringt Lob und Preis dem Höchsten dar,	Bring your praises to the Highest,
Dem Lamme, das getödtet war !	To the Lamb Who once was slain !
Halleluja :	Hallelujah !
Das siegreich aus dem Grab hervor	Who victorious from the grave
Sich hebet im Triumph empor	Goes in triumph up on high.
Halleluja ! Halleluja !	Hallelujah ! Hallelujah !
Ja lasst des Bundes Harfe klingen,	Let our harps in concert ring,
Dass Freude durch die Seele bebt !	Joy through every spirit thrill !
Lasst uns dem Sieger Kronen bringen,	To the Victor crowns now bring
Der auferstand und ewig lebt.	Who arose and lives for aye.
Bringt Lob und Preis, &c.	Bring your praises to the Highest, &c.
Lobsinget alle Himmelsheere !	Praises sing, all Heavenly hosts !
Dem Herrn sei Ruhm und Herrlichkeit !	Praise and glory to the Lord !
Anbetung, Macht und Kraft und Ehre	Worship, might, and pow'r and praise
Von Ewigkeit zu Ewigkeit !	Be to Him for evermore !
Bringt Lob und Preis, &c.	Bring your praises to the Highest, &c.

Woodfall & Kinder, Printers, 70 to 76, Long Acre, London, W.C.

ImTheStory.com

Personalized Classic Books in many genre's

Unique gift for kids, partners, friends, colleagues

Customize:

- Character Names
- Upload your own front/back cover images (optional)
- Inscribe a personal message/dedication on the
  inside page (optional)

Customize many titles Including
- Alice in Wonderland
- Romeo and Juliet
- The Wizard of Oz
- A Christmas Carol
- Dracula
- Dr. Jekyll & Mr. Hyde
- And more...

Emily's Adventures in Wonderland

Ryan & Julia

ISBN: 9781313605465

Published by:
HardPress Publishing
8345 NW 66TH ST #2561
MIAMI FL 33166-2626

Email: info@hardpress.net
Web: http://www.hardpress.net